# International Law and International Relations

James Kenneth Stephen

# INTERNATIONAL LAW

AND

# INTERNATIONAL RELATIONS.

AN ATTEMPT TO ASCERTAIN THE BEST METHOD OF DISCUSSING THE TOPICS OF INTERNATIONAL LAW.

BY

J. K. STEPHEN, B.A.

OF THE INNER TEMPLE, BARRISTER-AT-LAW.

London:

MACMILLAN AND CO.

1884

## NOTE.

The following essay is a dissertation which I wrote last year as a candidate for a Fellowship at King's College, Cambridge. Except in so far as it deals with the theory of International Law it is necessarily a mere sketch, as my object was only to state a theory and to give an outline of its application. It has interested some of its few readers sufficiently to encourage me to publish it. I have not amplified it at all because I can see no value in any work occupying an intermediate position between an essay intended to excite interest in the subject and to indicate what might be done and an elaborate work on International Law such as I may hope to write some day but for which much time and labour would be required. At the same time I have revised the essay and made some alterations in it. Its nature and purpose are further explained in the introductory letter which was prefixed to it in its earlier form and which I here reprint.

*Nov.* 1884.

## INTRODUCTION.

TO THE HON. MR JUSTICE STEPHEN, K.C.S.I.

MY DEAR FATHER,

I wish to preface this essay by an explanation of the relation of its contents to what you have written on International Law: and I think I can best make such an explanation in the form of an introduction addressed to you personally, and inviting your assent to the application which I have tried to make of your teaching. In the XVIth Chapter of the *History of the Criminal Law of England* you have occasion to deal with the subject of International Law in connection with the places and persons to whom the English criminal law applies. The passage dealing with the application of "International Law" to the case of R. *v.* Keyn (vol. II. pp. 34—37), and the reprint of your separate report on the Fugitive Slaves Commission (pp. 44—58), contain the matters to which I particularly refer. They explain and defend two positions: first, that the collection of usage and opinion to which the name "International Law" is conventionally applied, is not in fact at all similar to law properly so called: and secondly, that many of the topics of "International Law" are proper subjects for real laws, and that such laws can be enforced by civilised governments in places and against persons outside their normal jurisdiction. The first of these opinions involves disapproval of the usual method of writers on International Law: the second appears to me to suggest an alternative method for the discussion of the same topics. The object of this essay is to show how this alternative method might be applied to the whole subject, and might free it altogether from the theory involved by the use of the term "International Law."

When we speak of the prohibition of contraband trade, or the adoption of the three-mile limit, as instances of municipal legislation, we are confining ourselves to demonstrable facts, and leaving on one side the difficult questions of the effect upon these matters both of abstract morality and of the doubtful usages and opinions denoted by the name "International Law." Can we not adopt a similar course with regard to those topics of International Law which are not matters for municipal legislation, and which therefore do not come within the scope of a work on any branch of positive law? Can we not, that is, see what is the true character of those international relations which are in no way concerned with law, and show that they may be discussed in general terms, and at the same time called by their right names?

In the first part of this essay I have criticised at length the use of the expression International Law. Writers on International Law differ very much in their theoretical views and in details of method: but they all agree in the assertion of a common theory which must be used to support any juridical treatise on International Relations. That theory has often been attacked by those who believe in Austin's analysis of the leading terms of jurisprudence. Whatever else a "rule of International Law" may be, it is not a command addressed by a political superior to a subject, and it cannot be enforced by any sanction which would come within the terms of Austin's definition. Austin himself prefers the expression International Morality to International Law: and those who accept his teaching have often expressed dissatisfaction with the current theory of International Lawyers.

Such attacks however have usually consisted in brief and general denunciations and have not been accompanied by any attempt to show what could be substituted for it. The theory has been constantly adopted even by those who have plainly seen its defects, and the defences put forward on its behalf have been as elaborate as the criticisms against it have been scanty and contemptuous.

I have attempted to criticise the common theoretical views about International Law with some fulness of detail, and for that purpose I have selected the theoretical part of the writings of two particular authors. I have given the reasons for that selection in the body of the essay. I thought it better to attempt a comparatively full criticism of two representative writers than to give a cursory glance at the theories of many. In the second part I have tried to show how the field of International Law might be adequately covered by a discussion based on a sound theory.

In other words, I have tried to find a methodical arrangement for the well-known questions of "international law" according as they are either the subject of positive law, or else the subject of some other kind of sequence and arrangement which can be easily recognised and accurately described. I have not attempted to go into much detail, and I do not pretend to have anything of novelty or importance to say about any of the vexed questions of International Law. I have only tried to give an outline of a book which should deal with the topics of "International Law" from the point of view of the theory of which I advocate the adoption. This essay is nothing more than the vindication of a theory. Where it is a matter of dispute which of two views of a practical question is correct, I accept one view or the other for the sake of saying how I think it ought to be expressed and where it would find its place in such a work as that of which I am sketching the outline.

These introductory remarks are addressed to any one who may read my essay: but I have addressed them directly to you for the reasons which I have given. You will, I hope, allow me to consider this introduction as a dedication also: for I am sure that the value of what follows may be accurately measured by the extent to which it illustrates your opinions or secures your approval.

I am,

Your affectionate Son,

J. K. STEPHEN.

# PART I.

## INTERNATIONAL LAW.

THE object of the first part of this Essay is to criticise in detail the theoretical view which I propose to attack, and to explain the nature of the theoretical view which I wish to maintain.

International Law is the name which has been given to the science whose expositors have dealt with the alleged rights and duties of States towards other States, with regard to the three conditions of peace, war and neutrality.

It is approximately possible to give an account of all the conceivable relations between States, which may be spoken of as International Relations: to show the principles upon which these relations may be divided into classes: and to establish whether by historical induction or by *a priori* reasoning the actual nature, the relative importance, and the connection one with another of these classes. There is therefore a definite sense in which we may speak of a science of International Relations: and this science may be the subject of investigation and publication.

Such a science has in fact been put together and enunciated; its text-books circulate widely: it has had professors all over Europe: it has been pursued both inductively and deductively: its students have been numerous, acute, inventive and voluminous. The name which has been given to it is International Law.

"People have been found," an international lawyer will often say with some indignation at the outset of his treatise, "to deny that there is any such thing as international law:" and he proceeds to show that they have come to that conclusion on inadequate grounds, and that a few trifling defects have led them to reject a valuable and beneficent system. But people who deny the existence of international law do not therefore deny the existence of a science of International Relations. They say that the science has been misnamed: and that this misnomer has had practical effects which are to be regretted; that it has led to the study of international relations on a wrong basis: has led both governments and subjects to look at their neighbours in an artificial light: has needlessly embittered national controversies: and has perhaps prevented the establishment of a more useful science.

The object of this Essay is to support the view of those who deny the existence of international law in the sense in which such a denial has just been explained: and to show that the use of elaborate juridical metaphors in the scientific discussion of international relations has been an unfortunate mistake. But this is not enough: the objections to the employment of the terms of private law in a discussion of relations between persons who are subject to no sovereign and liable to no sanction have been often enumerated. But the antagonists of the common method of speaking have too often stopped here. Contented with showing that international relations can only be governed by international morality, they have not gone on to show that international morality is susceptible of really scientific treatment. Those who assert the existence of international law can retort that such criticism is at best purely destructive, and has nothing to offer in the place of what it destroys. They can urge that no human science is absolutely faultless in its method and results: and that in default of any competing system the system known as International Law should continue to be the standard science of international relations.

I shall attempt to show in outline how every department of the field of international relations might be adequately discussed in a science which should dispense altogether with juridical metaphor: how an account of these relations might be given in which everything should be called by its right name and where no recourse should be had to untrustworthy hypotheses. It will be my object to show that the use of the proposed method would be productive of that accurate classification and systematic completeness which distinguishes a science from a group of undigested empirical maxims. Such a science would assist the writer or the student of the history of international relations. It would enable any one who was acquainted with it to enter readily and intelligently into the study of a crisis in the relations between the great powers of the present day. In these ways it might perform a function similar to that of the science founded by Adam Smith. It would be full of suggestions, explanations and classifications; and these would be quite as useful for practical purposes as assertions that the nations of Europe are amenable to the jurisdiction of a shadowy tribunal, which administers a law as distinct as the oracles of Delphi and enforces it with an authority too indefinite to be compared to that of a modern suzerain.

It is easy to understand why the science of

International Relations has gone by the name of International Law and why its professors have delighted to talk about legal and illegal, penalty and judgment, or culprit and crime, although there is no tribunal to decide between nation and nation, and no definite penalty for misdeeds except that of war which is not certain to follow and which may prove highly beneficial to the wrongdoer. Hardly any one will deny that there is such a thing as good conduct and such a thing as bad conduct for the governments who act in the name of States: and when international quarrels arise and the world at large begins to question men of science as to the rights of the case it is this aspect of rightness or wrongness which is the most prominent aspect of international relations. When the science of International Relations is popular and commands many students, it is as a science of right and wrong that it wins popularity and attention. Its professors necessarily find themselves imposing duties, asserting rights, defining crimes and assessing penalties.

Since then national virtue and vice actually exist, it is natural that the temptation to throw the science of International Relations into a legal form and to make it a branch of Jurisprudence has not been resisted. Among individual men the most effective method of practically repressing crime and encouraging self-restraint and good faith has been the establishment of tribunals: the formation and in some cases the codification of law to be administered by such tribunals: and the elaboration of devices for utilizing the authority of the sovereign or government of States on behalf of their decisions or awards. Hence the favourite method of theoretically discussing any phenomena connected with the rightness and wrongness of human conduct has been to rely on legal and magisterial imagery for the system on which the science of such phenomena may be constructed. This habit has given their character to many religious and to many ethical systems. Accordingly Grotius, impelled to a scientific discussion of international relations by his indignation at particular kinds of national misconduct and by his desire for the establishment of a higher international morality, gave to the science which he founded the legal tone which it has never lost. In the midst of his collection of evidence as to customs, of expressions of personal opinion and quotations of the opinions of others, and of ingenious applications of passages from the Digest or the Code and their commentators, he never loses sight of his central theory on which the whole work depends. This theory is that the nations of Europe are to be regarded as persons living together somewhat as men live together in a single nation, subject to the same social instinct, and similarly amenable to law. This idea has struck root firmly among the countless successors of Grotius, has given their tone and shape to the standard works on International Law, has been grudgingly accepted by those to whom it is least satisfactory, and is responsible for the fact that some of the latest, most learned, and most elaborate of the scientific treatises on international relations are thrown into the form of a Code.

If it be granted, as it has been granted for the purposes of this Essay, that international morality exists, there may of course exist, and certainly no one can absolutely deny that there does exist, an international code: in other words all conceivable duties of one State towards another, or the things that a perfectly virtuous government would do or abstain from doing in its relations with its neighbours might be systematically stated for the edification of mankind. It is not particularly likely that such a statement will ever be made: if it were made its identity might not be recognised; and if its identity were recognised its precepts might be disregarded. So far the students and professors of International Law have differed widely from one another in their conclusions as to the conduct to be pursued in certain emergencies by the ideally perfect State: and even where the majority of persons interested in international problems do seem to agree that a particular "publicist" has solved a question of international duty, no one would be rash enough to affirm with certainty that the sovereigns of Europe will always do what it has been authoritatively laid down by a gifted author with the applause and consent of a convinced majority that they ought to do. However, doubtful as the actual existence of any of its articles may be, and in spite of the slightness of its compulsory power, an undiscovered or partly discovered international code in the sense just given to the words may be said to exist: and as everybody wishes to a greater or less extent that what ought to be done should be done, all students of international relations are more or less actuated by a desire that the international code should be gradually dragged out of obscurity, displayed in its dazzling entirety to the nations of the world, generally and thankfully acknowledged to be what it professes to be, and universally obeyed.

Let it be taken as proved then that our studies if wisely and successfully conducted will lead to the discovery of a code systematically enunciating the rights and duties of nations, and comparable in form to the codes by reference to which governments decide the questions which arise between individual subjects or between themselves and their subjects. Does it follow from this that we ought at once to draw up codes however imperfect? that we ought to borrow the style and language of legislators and jurists? that where we find a law made by a single State for the government of its subjects or even of persons not its subjects in respect of international relations, or an agreement between several governments on similar topics which is drawn up something like an Act of Parliament, we should incorporate these as they stand into our code of rules regulating the mutual relations of nations? and that any discovery of the real nature and bearing of international morality should be at once utilized as a clause in the international code? Or on the other hand should we merely lay down that such and such feelings are entertained on the subject of particular international relations? that particular governments have made such and such laws for the international conduct of their subjects and sometimes of other persons? that such and such international agreements have been made from time to time? and that such and such international effects (which anybody would approve of or which anybody would deplore but which few might at once foresee) will—to judge from analogy and history—follow such and such international causes? and shall we, as far as the international code is concerned, confine ourselves to hoping that its nature will be gradually discovered, and its objects to some extent secured by such inductive treatment of the science of international relations: just as the actual ethical code may be discovered in time by scientific investigations quite distinct from the temporary codification of legislatures, which have to meet particular problems in the interim and which are furnished for that purpose, as sovereign powers, with a kind of machinery to which nothing in the international system at all accurately corresponds?

It is the contention of this Essay that the former of these two opposed courses has been erroneously pursued and that the latter of them might be beneficially pursued.

In order to state the contrast between these two methods it will be necessary to say a little more about the general character of such sciences as deal with any department of human conduct. We have said already that the existence of international morality, or the applicability of the terms right and wrong to the conduct held towards each other by the corporations and officials whose duty is to represent nations, may be taken for granted. We may leave to students or professors of Ethics the definition of the terms right and wrong. We need not inquire into the nature of the standard of right and wrong: nor whether an absolute standard exists. But if and in so far as such a standard does exist we assume that it applies to international conduct. We may go farther and admit that an international "Duty to my Neighbour" might be drawn up: and that if it were of a sufficiently general character its truth would probably be admitted by all civilized nations. But the enunciation and general acceptance of the "Duty to my Neighbour" of the English catechism in a highly civilized community would hardly compensate for the want of regular civil and criminal law: and a group of individuals might admit its truth and declare conscientiously that their conduct was in conformity with it, and might yet from time to time have recourse to litigation, or in the absence of regular tribunals, to a vindication of their rights by force. The admission that the words good and evil apply to international conduct brings us to a difficulty which must necessarily be faced by the scientific student of international relations. Although there is no necessity for expressing every international relation as nearly as possible in terms of jurisprudence, such as right, duty and law, it is nevertheless impossible to take a comprehensive view of international relations without considering some cases of international conduct in which the moral aspect is more important than any other. We do not admit that all international relations ought to be classified with reference to international right, but we shall have to classify somehow among the rest those relations which spring from international wrong-doing or from international benevolence. It would be possible to set before us an object of scientific study International Right and Wrong or the Science of international relations as they ought to be: but we prefer to take as the subject of such study International relations as they are and to speak of International right and wrong incidentally, and in a manner appropriate to the inevitable vagueness and uncertainty by which the topic is surrounded.

The choice to be made between these two methods of dealing with International law illustrates the general distinction between the sciences of what is and the sciences of what ought to be. Among the departments of human knowledge which can form the subject of a science there are several which consist in human conduct: and with regard to each of these this distinction is important. Take first the science of human conduct as a whole: it is possible on the one hand to aim at setting out in a scientific classification all the kinds of conduct which exist: to discuss in a scientific spirit all the kinds of things that men have done and what they are likely to do under particular circumstances: it is possible on the other hand to aim at a statement of the standard of right and wrong and at its application to human conduct in general. There are thus possible the two sciences of what is and of what ought to be the behaviour of the human race as a whole. The same distinction exists if we take as the subject of a science not the whole of human conduct but a part of it. For instance we may consider the science of law: the laws which have been observed and enforced from time to time in the world with more or less success are the result of human conduct, either of the declarations of lawgivers, themselves to some extent the agents of public opinion, or of repeated habits and actions of a number of persons which have gradually constituted a custom: and the reaction of laws upon human conduct which created them is their most important and most interesting function. In the scientific study of law then (leaving customary law, which might be considered in the same way, for the moment out of sight) we can ask either what legislators have done, and how their action has affected mankind, or on the other hand what legislators ought to do and how their actions ought to affect mankind.

The science of law as it is will facilitate the study of any particular legal system by those who are to practise it: and the science of law as it ought to be will assist the labours of legislatures. Both will of course replace a portion of human ignorance by knowledge. Therefore each of these sciences has its distinct sphere of usefulness: but the science of law as it ought to be has perhaps never been separately and systematically studied: and the science of law as it is, has too often been mixed up with considerations of law as it ought to be. From the time when Ulpian preluded the discussion of the minutiae of Roman law by the statement that a law of nature prescribed the breeding of animals, we have had innumerable treatises on law as it is, or even on particular systems of law, which have been rendered confused and obscure by the introduction of statements of the law of nature or of law as it ought to be—clauses of a code whose complete discovery would be the gradual work of a science which has seldom been systematically pursued from the beginning.

Now the science of international relations is but a science dealing with a particular department of human conduct. Therefore the same distinction necessarily exists, and international conduct as it is, and international conduct as it ought to be are alike capable of scientific discussion. It is desirable that statesmen should have access to a compendious summary of the kinds of things that governments have done in their relations with other governments, and of the effects which have followed international causes: and it is also desirable if there is an abstract standard of good and evil international conduct capable of enunciation that it should be enunciated and so applied as to make a code. The result of the successful study of both branches of the science of international conduct might ultimately be their fusion in one. But it is obvious at least that the study of what ought to be the international relations of the nations of Europe is not identical with the study of what their actual relations have been: and although these distinct studies might be expounded in different parts of the same treatise, it is possible that the best and most profitable division of labour would be to assign the absolute duties and rights of nations to the students of the general science of what ought to be done, and to leave as the subject-matter of the science of international relations the actual conduct of nations in the past, present, and future, including the feelings likely to be aroused in individuals, or in nations by any particular sort of international conduct.

Now the study of international relations under

the name of International Law, and the adoption of that legal imagery against which this Essay is particularly directed, are liable to this among other objections:—that they have led to a confusion of the science of what nations do with the science of what nations ought to do, precisely similar to the confusion which has diminished the value of so many great works of jurisprudence. Following the example of Grotius, the students of this science have always spoken in the language of jurists: and in so doing they have introduced into their science the greatest error which has befallen the science of law. They have not kept international habits and international duties sufficiently distinct. Having by their choice of language and method had recourse to international laws, international codes, international tribunals and international penalties, so called by analogy to the legal phenomena to which these names have been given, they have added confusion to inaccuracy by mixing up the statement of the customs and facts which they classify by the help of these metaphors, with the items of abstract international duty which would be better understood and explained as the subject-matter of a separate science or of part of a separate science: and just as we have the Roman lawyers mixing together the statement of legal duties which sovereigns have imposed and which courts will enforce, and of moral duties, resulting from the nature of things and perceived by the subtle but fallible ingenuity of the writers themselves; so we have Hautefeuille[1] in his works on International Law giving us the Primary Law imposed by God, and engraved on the heart of every human being, side by side with the Secondary Law which contains detailed rules extracted from treaties and State papers and a kind of tertiary law which has apparently been engraved particularly clearly on the heart of M. Hautefeuille himself: and confounding in a common anathema those who have infringed any part of his composite code.

But it is not necessary to confine our search for these unfortunate results to the works of an author over whom Historicus made merry at the time of the American Civil War and whose *a priori* assertions will be rejected by the great majority of English readers. It will be better to take some of the best and most established authors on international law and see if the value of their books is not greatly impaired by the adoption of the legal metaphor: both on account of the necessary defects of a metaphor dependent upon so slight an analogy, and because of the par-

[1] *Droit Maritime International* (2nd edition, 1869) and other works of M. L. B. Hautefeuille.

ticular confusion between rules which are exhibited as specimens, and rules which are enunciated *ex cathedra* for the benefit of mankind,—a confusion from which all kinds of legal science have suffered, and to which this particular kind of quasi-law is also liable.

Let us then first consider the work of the late Professor Bluntschli, which is an example of the best that the theory of "international law" can do for the study of international relations. The third edition of his Code of International Law was published in 1878: the title of the book is *Das moderne Völkerrecht der civilisirten Staten als Rechtsbuch dargestellt*, and it consists of an introduction and of 862 short articles with explanatory notes giving shortly and clearly what the Professor considers to be the existing law on almost every international question that can arise. Let us see what Dr Bluntschli has to say in favour of the adoption of the method and language of jurists in the scientific discussion of international relations.

He sets out, at the beginning of the introduction, by stating that all men who live in intercourse with one another are necessarily gifted both with *Rechtsinn* and with *Rechtsgefühl*[1]: i.e. with the sense

[1] I have commented at length on the word *Recht* in the text. *Rechtsinn* appears to mean the capacity of being logically convinced of rules founded on *Recht*: *Rechtsgefühl* an instinc-

of right and with the instinct of right. When we consider the wide meaning of the word *Recht* we must take this to mean that men are necessarily inclined both by reason and instinct to recognise the existence of right and wrong, and also the fact that right conduct is conduct in accordance with some standard which is enunciated in the imperative mood by God or by nature or by the human race, and which is capable of similar enunciation by a sovereign legislature. Such being the nature of man as a reasoning and as an instinctive being, it follows that the State also which is a determinate aggregate of men is a *Rechtswesen*, or a being necessarily recognising the existence of *Recht*. *Völkerrecht* then, or the Right which can be expressed in commands addressed to States, is the summary of those duties of which States are cognisant just as individual men are cognisant of the numerous duties more or less adequately asserted by the laws of various States.

These preliminary assertions then come to no more than a statement of the existence of international morality, connected (by the use of the word *Recht*) with the fact that morality where its nature is fully understood can be expressed in the

tive readiness to perceive them. Bluntschli says that all human beings possess both: but that the former is especially characteristic of men, the latter of women.

form of commands, and that these commands are of a kind which can, subject to circumstances, be enforced in the shape of laws.

At this early point in his argument Blunstchli turns aside to deal with those who deny the existence of *Völkerrecht* (i.e. of International Law in the sense of a standard of international right and wrong which can be legally enunciated). It has been urged, he says, that it is inaccurate to speak of *Völkerrecht* because there is no *Völkergesetz*, and no *Völkergericht*—i.e. no regularly enacted and promulgated law for the regulation of national conduct and no tribunal for the enforcement of such law: and because nations are practically living in a state of anarchy, where might is right and the strongest can have his way. Dr Bluntschli admits that this criticism is based on real and serious defects in International Law: but he does not consider that these defects are at all sufficiently serious to justify the conclusions drawn from them and he shows their insufficiency by commenting upon them to the following effect.

When we want to know the law (*Recht*) on any question of inheritance &c., says he, we take down a *Gesetzbuch*—(a Code, a volume of the Statutes, or of the Law Reports)—and we see what has been enacted or laid down on the subject:

and the want of a *Gesetzbuch*, or absolutely authoritative exposition of *Recht* in international questions, is considered by some to disprove the existence of *Völkerrecht*. But in truth, says Dr Bluntschli, Laws (*Gesetze*) are not the only expression of the Law (*Recht*) but its clearest expression: and when any system of *Recht* is in its infancy (as the private law of every people has been at some period or other) we cannot expect to find this clearest kind of expression, and must be content with something less precise and satisfactory. One difficulty of course is the want of an international legislator (*Gesetzgeber*): but who knows? the "organisation of the world" is perhaps not so far off as we might think, and in the future mankind will become aware of its existence as a corporate being (*Gesammtwesen*) and, the world once organised, there will be no further difficulty about the establishment of an authoritative *Weltgesetz*, properly enunciated and enforced. But Dr Bluntschli admits that this lofty aim may be regarded as a "beautiful dream" though every improvement in international conduct is a step towards its realisation, and he proceeds to give some more practical answer to the critics who rely on the want of a *Gesetzgeber* and a *Gesetzbuch*. Although there be no regular legislator and no authoritative statement of the particular applications of *Völkerrecht*, yet there are:—(1) International congresses which profess to do something more than make mutual engagements for the regulation of international relations,—i.e. to lay down the true and valid principles which obtain with regard to particular relations, and to enunciate in a legal form the result of the application of those principles. The great powers of Europe do not say, we, *A*, *B*, *C*, *D* and *E* will not in making war upon one another employ privateers: but they say "Privateering is and remains abolished:" and if, on a question of this sort any powers refuse at once to conform to the principle laid down, they will soon be shamed into compliance. (2) Codes of particular States for the regulation of the international conduct of their subjects, especially the "Instructions for the Government of Armies of the United States in the Field"[1]: i.e. law-books or *Gesetzbücher* for individual States, which can be referred to by other States as a fairly trustworthy clue to the dictates of true international law (*Völkerrecht*). (3) Works in which private individuals like Dr Bluntschli himself collect and formulate as much international law or *Völkerrecht* as they can, and give to the world a *Rechtsbuch* which approximates very nearly to what the international *Gesetzbuch* would be if the want of

[1] See below, p. 122.

an international tribunal did not unfortunately prevent it from existing. "Animated by the American example," says Dr Bluntschli, "I have undertaken the task of drawing up such a *Rechtsbuch* of *Völkerrecht.*—If my exposition corresponds to the existing *Rechtsbewusstsein* (conscience in matters of *Recht*) of the civilised world and serves to explain and enunciate it, the object of this work is fulfilled: if not I only wish that another may soon be more successful in satisfying this reasonable want." And in a note to the second edition he mentions the wide popularity of his work and its translation into six languages as a proof that international law has at least a *Rechtsbuch* which can fulfil some of the functions of a *Gesetzbuch.*

As with the want of a *Völkergesetz*, so with the want of a *Völkergericht:* it is true that any system of *Recht* which has reached its highest development will be enforced by a regular tribunal precisely and effectively. But where development is less complete there are other less effective and less precise methods of enforcing *Recht.* Among the existing means by which the defect of a *Völkergericht* is supplied Dr Bluntschli mentions two: war and arbitration. While he admits that war is a rough and ready means of settling national disputes and that it is very likely to settle them wrong, he points out that "it is never a matter of indifference on which side Right is." The belligerent which has right on its side fights with a better conscience and greater belief in its cause, and therefore with a better chance of success than the nation which is in the wrong: those who are in the right have the support and applause of mankind, and those who are wrong meet with general disapproval: and in both these ways war is more likely to serve the good cause than the bad, and is therefore a tolerable substitute for a *Völkergericht* as an institution by which *Völkerrecht* can be enforced. With regard to arbitration it is an undeniable fact that important international quarrels have been submitted to arbitration and that the awards of the arbitrators have been accepted by the parties to whom they were unfavourable.

Dr Bluntschli winds up his answer to those who deny the existence of *Völkerrecht* by showing that the rule of force among nations is only imaginary, and that although violence has necessarily played an important part in European history, yet there has always been a tendency towards quiet and order: peace is now the rule and war the exception, whereas the opposite was once the case, and in war itself humanity and a respect of the rights of private property and of neutrals has taken the place of indiscriminate cruelty and rapacity.

The general and particular facts made use of by Dr Bluntschli in the argument just summarised are of course obvious and patent facts in connection with international relations: and it is on them that any argument as to the best theoretical method of treating of international relations must be founded. In trying to show that the facts really lead to a conclusion as to that method quite different from that arrived at by Dr Bluntschli we are met at once by a great difficulty. This difficulty is the vague and wide meaning of the word *Recht.* If we say that such arguments are sufficient to prove that these facts are consistent with the non-existence of international law we may be told that we are only proving the absence of a *Völkergesetz* which Dr Bluntschli regretfully admits. On the other hand if the word *Recht* is construed according to another of its possible grammatical meanings, the assertion that *Völkerrecht* exists is no more than an assertion of the existence of international morality which we have already agreed to take for granted. But notwithstanding the difficulties connected with this dangerously elastic substantive, the point at issue is a real one. In the brief statement that *Völkerrecht* does exist and in his argument against those who deny its existence,

Dr Bluntschli is doing something more than asserting the existence of international morality. If by the existence of *Völkerrecht* he does not mean that nations are subject to a law formally enacted and enforced, it is also true that he does not mean merely that it is possible for nations to do wrong in the most general sense of the term. He means at least as much as this: that the conduct of nations is subject to *Recht* so nearly comparable to the *Recht* which governs individuals, that it may be most accurately and profitably discussed by a science which treats international morality as if it had in a perfect form those sanctions and those legislative enactments which it at present lacks: and that the general statement and arrangement of a science of international relations should closely resemble a practical treatise on the law by which any civilised State is governed. Upon this construction of Dr Bluntschli's assertion of the existence of *Völkerrecht*, a construction which is borne out by the actual character of his own book, we proceed to deal with the arguments which we have summarised.

Congresses certainly meet from time to time, and among other things they make declarations touching the subject-matter of the science called international law. But, although the form of these declarations may vary, and may at times approximate closely to that of legislative formulae, they can never in fact be anything but clauses of a treaty to which a greater or less number of powers are parties. Instances can be found in European history to show that treaties are not always binding upon the powers which agree to them. The same treaty of 1856 which is looked upon as the great instance of international legislation, contained provisions as to the navigation of the Black Sea which were dispensed with less than 20 years later by one of the contracting parties, on the ground that observance of them was inconsistent with the development of that power. The fact that this step gave rise to another declaration by treaty that declarations by treaty were to be considered binding on those who made them, is at least as good evidence of the weakness as it is of the strength of this species of *Völkergesetze.*

If the binding force of treaties upon those who make them is to be understood to be thus limited, their strength to bind outside powers must be small indeed. Dr Bluntschli speaks of the power which retains an obnoxious usage being ashamed to employ it in warfare against a power which has abandoned it. In Magna Charta it was enacted that foreign merchants who were in England at the outbreak of war should be treated as the

English merchants in the foreign country were treated: not that a good example should be set by treating them as friends. And ever since in respect of various kinds of international questions, and especially in the great dispute as to neutral rights which reached its highest point some 80 years ago, and which finally took the shape of a competition between England and Napoleon as to which could devise a policy the most oppressive to neutrals, it has been more common for nations to follow a bad example on the principle of reciprocity than to persist in setting a good one until it is followed through shame.

It has yet to be seen whether the privileges obtained by neutrals in 1856 would be safe in a great maritime war. If any of the signing powers broke any of their engagements, the principle of reciprocity would be likely to make itself felt: and it would certainly require a steadfast and prolonged adherence to the treaty on the part of all the powers who had signed, to make the other powers act from motives of shame as if they had signed too. It is certainly rather sanguine, for instance, to hope that America upon war breaking out would give up privateering because it was "abolished" at the treaty of Paris, and that the English government would then forbid their ships to take private property at sea, because they would know that the concession about privateering was so very distasteful to the Americans as long as private property at sea was liable to capture.

The topic of treaties must be generally discussed hereafter: but I have tried to show that the occasional meeting of European congresses which sometimes adopt a legislative style, does not go very far to make up for the want of *Völkergesetze* and of a *Gesetzgeber*.

The American Instructions for the Government of Armies in the Field are no doubt of great value and importance[1]. But they only apply to a certain part of international duties: and there is nothing in them to impose a duty upon any other government to issue a similar set of regulations, or upon the American government to keep in force those which it has issued. An enactment or set of enactments made by any nation for the regulation of the conduct of its military and naval officers in time of war may contain provisions which are due to international considerations: but how can we say of any particular provision in such a treaty that it is not due to some purely local and transitory motive, which has reference only to the legislating government, and to that only at the present time?

[1] See a further discussion of them, p. 128.

To consider these Instructions as a substitute for international *Gesetze* (or laws in the narrowest sense of the word) is to use them for a purpose for which they are incomplete and to neglect, perhaps, another and a sounder use of them. A government can make laws for its soldiers and sailors as it can for any other section of the community. Such laws, like any other laws, may be made because of any one of an infinite number of motives present to the minds of the legislators. The motives for this kind of legislation will very largely consist in a feeling of humanity towards other nations, in a desire for the establishment of a system of warfare which shall best serve the general interest of mankind, and in fear of the practical consequences of that irritation of other nations to which a harsh and violent method of carrying on war might give rise. But the presence of these motives does not give to this particular class of laws, as compared with laws in general, any special obligation upon the subjects to whom they are addressed, nor does it impose on the legislators who have enacted them any special obligation not to revoke or to alter their own enactments. But if such enactments as the American Instructions are to be looked on as a substitute for *Gesetzbücher* as defined by Dr Bluntschli it ought to be either because all governments are under a practical obligation to issue identical instructions, or because the instructions once called into existence and published impose some valid obligation upon individuals apart from any obligation resulting from the sovereign authority of the legislative power.

Finally we have to consider Dr Bluntschli's argument that such works as his own, which are *Rechtsbücher* of international law, can practically supply the defect caused by the absence of *Gesetzbücher* or regular law-books stamped with legislative authority. An ideal law-book has this merit —that it is perfectly definite and unmistakeable, giving the very words in which the legislature or perhaps a high judicial tribunal has expressed itself on the matter at issue and rendering it unnecessary to reopen the question of absolute right: we need only ascertain the meaning actually attached to the words used, for these words were chosen as the best possible expression of the order which the government will enforce. Perhaps it may be said that all the kinds of books which Bluntschli refers to under the head of *Gesetzbücher* fall short to some extent of this ideal. But there must be some level at which a book falls so far short of it as not to be suitably comparable to it at all. Such books as Dr Bluntschli's appear to be necessarily below this level. A government is about to do an act on behalf of the nation: the act is one which has an effect upon international relations. Before they have decided whether to do it or not, an influential adviser of the government opens Dr Bluntschli's book: he finds a sentence expressed with the utmost precision and in the most definite terms, laying down that such actions as that proposed to be done are contrary to international law: he knows that this means that upon consideration of all that has been said and done in connection with the particular kind of conduct, and acting under the influence of his own character, feelings and nationality, Dr Bluntschli has come to the conclusion that such conduct is to be disapproved of and condemned. His examination of authorities may not in this particular case have been exhaustive: his weighing of the conflicting arguments may have been hasty or inaccurate: some personal characteristic or some of those national prepossessions from which the gravest and most abstract historians are not always free, may have warped his judgment: men of similar qualifications with the same materials at hand may about the same time have come to an opposite conclusion. If for any of the above reasons Dr Bluntschli has come to a wrong conclusion he does not possess that might by which a legislature can make the most wrong-headed and perverse conclusions to be right as far as its subjects are concerned. Taking all these facts into consideration, the adviser of the government will let the dictum of the Professor take its place among the other arguments which he has collected from one source and another, and give a tinge to the advice which he eventually proffers to the government. Perhaps he will advise the government that on the whole he thinks the proposed action morally objectionable, and that he thinks most people will agree with him. But even if he were right in both assertions it is possible that particular practical considerations might lead the government to take the morally objectionable course, and it is even conceivable that the national prosperity might never suffer on account of their having done so. Is the part played by an international law-book in such a conjuncture much like that played by a statute-book, digest or code to which an individual may refer before doing something which he suspects to be in the nature of a crime or of a civil wrong? Such a man would read in unmistakeable terms that such or such consequences were attached to the act by law: and however much he might disagree with the motives of the legislature, or think that they had misunderstood the question, his knowledge as to whether by doing the act he should become a person punishable by law or legally liable to pay damages would at once be absolute and complete. The analogy appears to be so slight as to point to the conclusion that the existence of such books as Bluntschli's *Rechtsbuch* does not supply the defect of regular law-books.

We now come to what Bluntschli calls the second defect of International Law: the absence of a regular tribunal to inflict a penalty for the breach of it or to determine the rights of a disputed question. It may fairly be said that this defect is in fact the same as the first. The reason why there is no authoritative exposition of international law is the absence of any power to decide international questions. Particular views on any question can be expressed with the utmost precision: but our difficulty is that we do not know which to select among these precise but contradictory assertions. If any of them were enunciated as those which tribunals could enforce the difficulty would be at an end. However Dr Bluntschli has told us that the decisions of Congresses, the American Instructions, and his own paragraphs will do for authoritative expositions: and now he tells us that war and arbitration will do well enough for tribunals. That is to say, that the dicta of the three authorities mentioned are to be interpreted as saying to the world at large, "Do this—or you will probably be beaten in war," and

"Abstain from that—or arbitrators will award damages against you." The facts that in Dr Bluntschli's opinion the victors in war are generally in the right, and that on certain occasions governments have submitted to arbitration and have accepted awards, hardly bring the relations of States into close analogy with those of individuals subject to law. The injured State may tamely submit to injury or if it fight it may possibly be beaten. The powerful malefactor may refuse to have recourse to arbitration or may reject the award and leave the matter after all at the discretion of that God of battles in whose equitable intervention the Heidelberg professor so devoutly believes. The nation which is defeated because it is in the wrong, or which agrees to arbitration, is not in a position closely analogous to that of the individual who is made to pay damages for breach of contract or for interference with his neighbour's rights by ordinary process of the law.

The whole matter is summed up by Dr Bluntschli's assertion that whatever things may have been in the past, nations are not now living in a state of anarchy, but in a state of law and order. No theoretical defence of the common method of discussing international relations can dispense with the comparison of individuals to nations; and it is implied in this assertion. Several

3—2

inconveniences must attend a comparison of things in some respect so unlike: but let us make the comparison. We must imagine a continent or large tract of land inhabited by eight or ten individuals, differing greatly in size and strength; not necessarily mortal though each is liable to fall to pieces, or to be absorbed by or willingly coalesce with another; subject to spasmodic increase and decrease, but not growing regularly; incapable of reproduction or multiplication in the ordinary way, though the partial or complete decomposition of an individual may give rise to the sudden appearance of one or more new individuals; self-sufficient for the necessities of life, though each can benefit much by dealing with the others.

The question is whether these eight or ten men are subject to law or in a state of anarchy. It is common ground that the ethical standard, whatever it be, does in fact apply to their conduct. But are they subject to law? or does the necessary obligation to do good and shun evil possess in their case that subtle analogy with law as ordinarily promulgated and enforced which justifies the use of the substantive *Recht?* The advocate of an affirmative answer to this question can only say of this little group that a few of them have sometimes met together and emphatically asserted that when they fight they will not hit each other below the belt, or take the opportunity of picking each other's pockets: that one of the most conscientious of them keeps private memoranda containing more detailed regulations for his own conduct when fighting with his neighbours: that shrewd observers have gone into the matter very carefully and drawn up complete expositions of what seem to them to be the rights and duties of these men towards each other: that when they fight the one who is in the right is for that reason the more likely to win: and that on some occasions two men who have quarrelled have been known to submit the matter to the arbitration of some of the others and to accept their award.

One may look upon these men as fairly polished and civilised individuals: but one could hardly say that they were living under laws or a Law upon any reasonable interpretation of the word, whether German or English. The reason why they have attained to a higher degree of civilisation than ordinary men do without becoming subject to law, is that they are so very different from ordinary men as to render the whole comparison ridiculous. We allow that the matters on which we are at issue with Dr Bluntschli may be brought to a point in the question whether nations live in a state of anarchy or not: and we contend that, upon our opponent's own showing, if they do not, no kind of men ever did or can live so: for the word *Recht* (as an attribute inconsistent with anarchy) must be used in a sense so wide as to include the unspecified and neglected obligations to behave rightly which exist for savages, and perhaps for wild animals.

Let us now turn to the theoretical views of another expositor of International Law, Mr Hall[1]. Dr Bluntschli is a good example of those who have heartily adopted the common view as to the scientific method of International Law, and have at the same time avoided extravagance and unnecessary sophistries in the use of it. Mr Hall is a good example of another class of writers,—those who adopt the common method to a very limited extent: who even so seem to adopt it reluctantly and with a regretful consciousness of its great defects; and whose exposition of the actual facts of international relations is so honest and accurate as to display the faultiness of their method at every turn. It will take very little space to show that Mr Hall is no enthusiastic advocate of a theory which he pares down to the utmost and whose defects are apparent throughout his book:

[1] Hall's *International Law*, Oxford, 1880.

but the important question remaining for decision is whether there is any alternative as to the method to be pursued. It is the object of this essay to answer in the affirmative this question to which Mr Hall seems to assume a negative answer.

"International Law," says Mr Hall, "consists "in certain rules of conduct which modern civilised "States regard as being binding on them in their re- "lations with one another with a force comparable "in nature and degree to that binding the con- "scientious person to obey the laws of his country, "and which they also regard as being enforcible "by appropriate means in case of infringement." And he then explains and defends the opinion that these rules are "a reflection of the moral "development of the external life of the particular "nations which are governed by them." Mr Hall is willing to leave altogether on one side any question as to the absolute standard of International right and wrong. He differs emphatically from those who would constantly refer current differences to this standard, and who would at once inscribe new-formed rules in the absolute code in which this standard is universally applied. He says that international law can only grow up as custom changes and as national life developes: that at any given moment it is what the conduct of nations has made it: that it cannot be changed by any legislative decree or prevented from changing by any dogmatic reiteration: and that we must find out how it applies to any particular problem by an examination of international usage, and a very delicate and cautious use of the materials afforded to us by treaties.

It may be admitted with Mr Hall that it is desirable to let the absolute standard alone for the present. But it does not necessarily follow that the best way of discussing international relations in a practical spirit, which is in fact what Mr Hall has done, is to write a treatise on "International Law" according to the above definition.

In the first place it is not easy to say what is the force which binds a conscientious person to obey the laws of his country. A conscientious person differs from other people only by being more awake than they to the promptings of conscience. The difficulty of defining "conscience" is great enough to leave us in some doubt if we were told merely that international law consisted of rules which impose an obligation on nations similar to the obligation on a conscientious man to do what his conscience bids him. But we have a more subtle distinction to deal with. What are the promptings of conscience as to the law of the land? That must depend to some extent on the character of the laws: for of course there may be a law so bad that conscience orders its violation. We must suppose then that in addition to the obvious moral obligation to obey good laws and disobey bad ones conscience imposes upon a man an amount of obligation not definable to obey his country's laws independently of the goodness or badness of particular laws, so that it will want a considerable amount of badness in a law to overcome the conscientious man's inclination to abide by law. But this obligation, of which the existence may undoubtedly be admitted, would seem upon analysis to depend upon the fact that it is desirable to maintain the administrative system of the country, to give the legislature fair play, and to direct reforming energy into constitutional channels. Therefore the obligation upon a conscientious man, *qua* conscientious man, to obey his country's laws seems to be intimately connected with those conditions of sovereign power, efficient tribunals, &c., whose absence in International Law Mr Hall would not deny. From this it seems to follow that governments are not bound to obey the rules of international law, independently of their actual merit according to a standard whether of morality or of expediency, as a man is bound by conscience to obey the laws of his country: and when Mr Hall says that "civi-"lised States regard these rules as binding on "them with a force comparable in nature and "degree" to the obligation which we have been discussing, it is no more than a way of saying that there is after all a slight analogy between international law and private law.

This is still more evidently the meaning of the statement that "civilised states regard (these rules) "as being enforcible by appropriate means in case "of infringement." Of course, if they were really enforcible and enforced by thoroughly appropriate and efficient means, there would be no need for the allusion to the conscientious man. The obligation would be the same as that which binds all men, conscientious or not, to keep their country's laws. At the same time we can hardly suppose that the modern civilised powers are taken to be under a delusion as to the extent to which these appropriate means exist. We must conclude that the intentional vagueness of the phrase points to the fact that international duties have been from time to time practically enforced: and that upon this side also there is a slight analogy to positive law.

With very little introductory matter beyond what we have quoted or summarised, Mr Hall proceeds to describe the "modern civilised states" with which he is dealing and then, first generally and afterwards in detail, to give an account of the law governing nations in their normal relations, in the relation of war and in the relation of neutrality. His method is, with regard to each kind of relations, to summarise the past and present usage of nations, showing what is obsolete and what is still authoritative, to analyse carefully the effect of such treaties as have been made touching the matter at issue, and in conclusion to give the existing rule of international law, or the rule, perhaps, which he perceives to be gradually forming; the rule, that is, which civilised modern nations regard (or soon will regard) as binding upon them with a force comparable in nature and degree to the indefinite inclination of the conscientious man to observe the laws of his country, and which they believe (or soon will believe) to be enforcible by appropriate means, if it should be infringed. When Mr Hall winds up a historical discussion of the "right" to navigate territorial rivers, or to carry enemy's goods under a neutral flag, and ends by enunciating the international "rule" now in force or in process of formation, we must remember the rather elaborate periphrasis implied by the use of the words "right" and "rule".

Such books as Mr Hall's may possess great merits as statements of European customs and as commentaries on European treaties: the study of them may throw considerable light on particular international complications. But the merits of such a book belong to it in despite of its theoretical method: and that method itself must be reckoned as a defect. The explanation of the theory on which the author proceeds is only a more or less ingeniously involved statement that international relations are the subject of a considerable number of rules which bear a slight analogy to the laws which regulate the conduct of individuals: and that in the absence of any competing theory, the existing knowledge on the subject of international relations had better be arranged and expressed in reference to that analogy. In order to meet the arguments by which such writers support their theory we need not enter into a detailed discussion like that demanded by the theoretical views of Bluntschli. We have to disprove not the existence of the analogy insisted upon, but its suitability to form the basis of a discussion of international relations. This will be done if we can show that any arrangement and mode of expression can be contrived resting on a clearer and firmer basis than the analogy of international rules to positive law.

All writers on International Law who have obtained much credit and authority since its original foundation, have made the alleged fact that nations are amenable to law the key-stone of their system. Those among them who have defended the assertion of this fact by elaborate argument can be met by such reasoning as that which has been here employed in criticising Dr Bluntschli: those who have spoken of the fact as a slight and doubtful one which they are constrained to use for want of a better theory on which to base their work can be met like Mr Hall by a demonstration that a scientific discussion of international relations is possible in which international rules are only considered as a particular class of international phenomena.

The above criticism of these two representative books arose from the assertion that the adoption of the juridical method must lead to a confusion of international habits with international duties, or the mixture of the science of international relations as they are with that of international relations as they ought to be. This confusion must exist in both classes of books if these criticisms are sound. For authors of one class assert more than they can prove about the existence of laws or a Law governing the relations of States to one another: and those of the other class set out with assertions which resolve themselves upon analysis into an admission that their science owes its arrangement and expression to the slight analogy existing between the relations of States and those of beings subject to positive law. Both classes therefore will be driven to look at non-juridical facts in a juridical light, and to describe those habits which are only rules in the sense of uniformity as habits which are rules in the sense of enforced uniformity. Exceptional incidents will be looked on as objectionable transgressions: and we shall never be certain whether our teachers are the exponents of a science of international relations as they are, or of that part of the science of ethics which refers to the conduct of nations as it ought to be. The alternative course here suggested is to treat of the forms and classes of international relations as they are, pointing out however that some relations are particularly apt to be looked on from one point of view or another as matters of morality, and that certain opinions as to right and wrong have in fact been maintained by eminent writers, or embodied (as hereafter explained) in municipal laws.

But we are not concerned only with this particular confusion. Before we pass from a criticism of these theories to a brief sketch of the application of a different one, we must look again and more generally at the way in which the theoretical views of the two authors who have been mentioned affect the practical character of their books. By this means we can ascertain more exactly the contrast between them severally and between each of them and the third theoretical stand-point which is about to be described.

That which is to be scientifically treated consists in the various international relations of which histories and newspapers give us an account. This account is necessarily in the nature of an unscientific inventory or catalogue because it follows the order of time and does not concern itself with the arrangement of different classes of relations according to their real nature. How do the theories of these two authors affect the treatment of the material or evidence at their disposal?

Bluntschli tells us of great moral principles which every State is morally bound to acknowledge whether it likes or not (§ 3), and which the various States of the world do acknowledge to a degree dependent on the development of their consciences, the development of consciences being the most important result of civilization (§§ 3, 4): these principles can be accepted by States of any religious views (§ 6) and without interference with national independence and individuality (§ 8): they cannot as yet be regularly embodied in international legislation (§ 10), but the language of the public documents of particular States in their dealings with others, and of the regular legislation of single States on a particular class of subjects (such as the conduct of armies in the field) can be deliberately founded on these principles and can help to propagate them (§ 12). The opinion of nations (*consensus gentium*) (§ 13) though it fluctuates, and the conduct of nations (§ 14), though sometimes unprincipled (§ 15), together with the published views of statesmen and philosophers (§ 16), will afford sufficient evidence of the actual nature of these principles. The historical matter, therefore, which is accessible to scientific inquirers is to be discussed and classified with reference to these principles which are morally binding on the conscience of the whole of mankind: and the result to be aimed at is the assertion of what is the right conduct to be pursued under all circumstances. Such assertions must necessarily fall into something like the form in which legislatures lay down what it is right for their subjects to do, in all those emergencies upon which the legislature has undertaken to enforce a rule.

Mr Hall on the other hand does not at all concern himself with eternal principles, binding on the human conscience at all times and at all places alike. He says that there are rules to some extent binding on a particular group of nations at the present time: that these rules are the reflection of national custom, with which they vary from time to time: and that they can be collected by a judicious study of national habits as they are and of the expressions given to the opinions by which statesmen believe or wish the nations whom they serve to be actuated. His treatment, therefore, of the material common to all international lawyers is governed by the wish to discover and enunciate the rules at this time vaguely binding the consciences of European and American statesmen in their intercourse with their neighbours: and the method, arrangement, and phraseology of his book are due to the nature of the attempt in which he is engaged.

The detailed criticism already made on the theoretical reasoning of these two authors is intended to justify the opinion that we may fairly take exception to the method and to the language of both. If that criticism is sound we may say with Mr Hall that we are quite willing to admit the existence of such principles as those described by Dr Bluntschli, but that their vagueness and the difficulty of agreeing as to their actual nature, render them unsuitable for the next few centuries at all events as the theoretical groundwork for a scientific study of international relations: but we may in the same way admit that the actual state of custom and opinion does impose an indefinite moral obligation on European and American statesmen to behave according to rules more or less accurately ascertainable, and at the same time say that even these rules are of too vague a kind to be set forth dogmatically as the result of a scientific discussion of international relations and therefore to give to such a discussion its tone and its method.

The unsuitability of the principles of right and wrong or of any kind of human rule, transient or eternal, as the dominant idea of this science appears not only from the vague nature of such principles or rules but also from the fact that some part of the acknowledged subject-matter of the science cannot possibly be put into the shape of rules, or stated at all definitely as an example of the working of a moral principle. Instances of this will be found in the sections where Dr Bluntschli deals with the difference between the rank of king and emperor or the kind of representatives to which different kinds of states are entitled. It can hardly be an exemplification of an eternal principle that "as a rule Ambassadors are only "sent and received by states of kingly rank" (172). And it would be difficult to illustrate the subjection of nations to Law by quoting provisions that an ambassador has no right to invitations or visits except those of which the absence would constitute an injury to the honour and to the acknowledged rank of his state (190), or that official correspondence must not be read by persons to whom it is not addressed (although it has always been found prudent to conduct such correspondence in cipher) (199).

We may reasonably prefer to take international relations as they are, and make such a methodical arrangement of them as their nature appears to suggest. If such an arrangement could be made so as to be complete and accurate it would assist every kind of students in their study of the history of international relations. Philosophers would arrive more easily at the great principles underlying international intercourse and national life: and those for whom the comparison of a nation to a particularly conscientious individual is especially interesting could also carry on their researches more expeditiously. All that is now urged amounts to this: that the everlasting principles on the one hand, and the indefinite transitory obligations on the other are not plain enough to be utilised as the basis of a scientific investigation: and that much of the matter to be investigated has no apparent connection either with the great principles or with the transitory obligations. If this is so, it will be a better employment of time and trouble to devise a scientific arrangement for such facts about international intercourse as are plain and undisputed. Where we find a book which so nearly approaches this result as Mr Hall's does, we are inclined to conclude that his insistance on the comparison of a nation to a conscientious individual subject to law, is an accidental result of the traditional method of international lawyers. But however slightly such a comparison be relied on it must impair the value of the book by making its contents the subject of dispute by those who differ as to the nature of an obligation which is so much obscured either by human prejudice and short-sightedness or by its own nature.

It is important to insist on the fact that the objection to basing the Science of International Relations on the idea of a Law of Nations is as much a practical as a theoretical one. The idea that nations are subject to law having been over popularised must lead to other feelings and inclinations besides those originally contemplated. International disputants with the idea of international law in their heads conduct their quarrels in a different spirit from that by which they would otherwise be actuated. They come to look upon the other party to the quarrel not as a community with which they have had a difference of opinion but as a being from whom they have suffered a legal wrong and from whom legal redress must be obtained. Hence arises a different aspect and possibly a regrettable embitterment of the quarrel. The ideas of the disputants are carried away from the actual facts of the case to the version of them as they appear in the light of the juridical metaphor. This is one practical objection to the current theory. Another is that the general belief in the existence of International Law is that municipal legislation on international subjects is neglected. It is imagined that the existence of courts whose duty is to administer the "law of nations" will be enough. The provisions of that law are allowed to reside "in gremio magistratuum". Codification by particular nations of their views on what the law of nations is, comes very slowly and in some departments does not come at all. Hence the differences of opinion which exist among different nations are not declared beforehand. They are only declared when an actual quarrel has arisen: and the discovery by a nation that its neighbour differs from it as to what the Law of Nations on some question is comes as an unpleasant surprise to embitter an existing dispute.

It may be said that any one who talks about a science of international relations is bound to admit the existence of laws which govern those relations, because a science is necessarily concerned with those laws which underlie all growth and govern every cause and effect in nature. To make a scientific statement is merely to publish a chapter of nature's laws, or to describe various instances of that uniformity by which one phenomenon is invariably connected with another. But it is fair to answer this by saying that the laws of this kind which govern international relations are not demonstrably such laws as Bluntschli declares to be binding on all the peoples of the world, and more or less obeyed by them according as they are more or less civilised: nor such as Mr Hall declares to be binding on the inhabitants of a particular group of nations with a force comparable in nature and degree to that binding the conscientious man to obey the laws of his country. We may admit that the scientific study of international relations will show some necessary connections of one thing with another, which could be compared with the so-called "laws" of physical science: but at the same time deny that it has ever been intelligibly proved that a scientific statement of the necessary connections between the observable peculiarities of mankind would constitute a suitable civil and criminal code either for eternity or for a few generations.

Having gone through the principal objections which I have to make to the reasoning on which the current theory is founded, and having described the most dangerous of its necessary evil results, I have now to give a brief account of the method by which I suggest that international relations might be more accurately and more beneficially discussed.

I propose to discard as a principal and immediate end the ascertainment of the moral rules by which nations are bound in their intercourse with one another: and to make the attempt to show in outline how the kinds of relations subsisting between them are a suitable subject for a theoretical analysis in which the solution of moral problems would hold a subordinate part. The first question which meets us in an attempt to consider the general theoretical characteristics of international relations is that of what we mean when we speak of nations.

I shall try to describe that one among the current uses of the word nation which is the best suited to bring into the field of international relations the kind of topics which are generally dealt with in works on "International Law". Having ascertained the meaning of the word nation, we shall be brought to consider the general characteristics and the historical career of the bodies of men so designated. We shall then know what are the chief characteristics of the political existence of the great societies with whose mutual relations we are concerned. We shall be led to think of nations rather as a particular class of political communities, to whom the course of history has bequeathed a miscellaneous collection of characteristics and instincts, than as great beings, into which the human race has been divided by nature for some purposes, and which are similarly subdivided for other purposes into smaller beings called men. Coming to the relations subsisting between nations we shall be occupied by the relations of peace, war and neutrality, and with regard to each of these we shall have to inquire what are the means by which international intercourse is carried on, what direction such intercourse generally follows, and what kind of questions arise between nation and nation.

Great political societies, independent of external control, possessed of vast wealth and resources, must now and then, in the course of their busy and active careers, be actuated by conflicting interests and view the conduct of one another with mutual disapprobation. The circumstances under which such feelings will arise, the results which will be likely to follow their manifestation, and the conflicting motives by which they are restrained, are all matters for investigation. These topics are none the less interesting because of their wide difference from the corresponding matters among individuals who are subject to the enactment and administration of regular law.

But while nations are not subject to laws from without, they are themselves provided with effective legislative and judicial organs. This fact is productive of many important effects upon international relations. It must therefore receive separate consideration, both in the general discussion of the nature of nations, and in the particular examination of the theoretical aspect of that part of a nation's conduct which affects its neighbours.

The second part of this Essay consists of a short sketch of the subject-matter of "International Law" as it would appear if discussed upon the principle here advocated. This sketch differs from what a similar abstract of any of the current books on International Law would be in two respects. First, it differs negatively because the usual ethical dicta as to what is right with regard to various international matters, or what the voice of the conscience of mankind would really say about them, are not to be found in it at all. Secondly, it differs both in the character of the preliminary descriptions of nations and national life, and in the arrangements of the ordinary topics of International Law. I hope that none of the latter are entirely absent, but they are mentioned in an order which depends on the arrangement here advocated, and not on the precedents of well-known text books.

The 1st, 2nd and 3rd sections state what is meant by those "nations" to which reference is implied by the use of the word "international" in the expression "International relations". The 4th section leads the way to that application of the Austinian conception of positive law to the phenomena of the intercourse of international intercourse which determines the arrangement of what follows. I have referred in the Introduction to that portion of the XVIth Chapter of my father's "History of the Criminal Law" in which this way of looking at "International Law" is described. The 5th, 6th and 7th sections deal with the various topics of International Law under the usual heads of Peace, War and Neutrality. Each of these sections is divided into two parts headed A. and B., the former dealing with such topics as are not, and the latter dealing with such as are usually subjects of municipal legislation.

The student of International Law will find the principal topics with which he is familiar mentioned under the following heads.

§ 3. A. Sovereigns in foreign territory.
Commercial Intercourse.

Dealings of individuals with foreign governments.
Diplomatic Intercourse.
Congresses, etc.
Treaties.

B. "Private International Law."
Naturalisation.
Nationality of ships.
Extradition.
Libel of foreign Sovereigns.
Conspiracies to commit crimes abroad.
Ambassadors and Consuls.
Jurisdiction and territorial waters.
"Exterritoriality" of ships.
Piracy.
The Slave Trade.
The right of search.

§ 6. A. Retorsion.
Reprisals.
Pacific Blockade.
Intervention.
Recognition of Independence.
Declaration of War.
Obligations of belligerent Sovereign towards hostile individuals and treatment of hostile individuals in belligerent territory at the outbreak of war.

B. Treatment of occupied territory.
Regular troops and irregular combatants.
Treatment of prisoners.

§ 7. A. Violation of neutral territory.
Neutral territory used as a base of operations.

B. Foreign Enlistment Acts.
Contraband.
Blockade.
Enemy's goods in neutral ships.
Neutral goods in enemy's ships.
Prize Courts.

## PART II.

## INTERNATIONAL RELATIONS.

### § 1. *Meaning of the word nation.*

CIVILISED men are divided into States, and there is a kind of State to which the name Nation may be applied. I use the word state in accordance with a common though not universal practice in a wider sense than nation: I use it as a generic term for independent political societies, and I use the word nation to designate those particular states to which it seems to me historically demonstrable that the applicability of "International Law" is confined. I use the word nation in this restricted sense because such a use of the word, while it can be justified by some among the many conflicting senses in which it is used, is particularly suitable for my purposes as enabling me to make a consistent use of the term "International" as an attribute of those relations which I am attempting to classify.

The scientific or theoretical discussion of international relations might form a branch of the general science of states. It happens to be convenient to take the relations which exist between nations as a separate subject apart from the internal character of states and from their relations to the individuals of whom they are composed. The fact that this is so is due to the actual history of a particular group of states and to the importance which has been already given to the theoretical or general character of the relations existing between them.

Nations then are the members of a particular group of states, whose relations it is convenient to discuss as the subject of a separate theory or science. A state is a community habitually subject to the government of a strong and stable sovereign body and practically or usually independent of external authority. A nation is a state belonging to a particular kind or at least to a particular group of states. The states called nations can be individually ascertained: but they have also, notwithstanding many differences, a general likeness to one another. This likeness is very difficult to describe fully, and can only be inferred from a comprehensive study of the states which are called nations: but to some extent it depends on the character of the tie by which their members are united.

The members of a community which forms a state are generally connected by some other tie besides that of submission to a common government. Community of language, community of religion and the consciousness of or belief in a common descent are among the most important of such ties. The tie which binds together the members of a nation is almost always compounded to some extent of each of these different ties: but particular importance is generally atached to the tie of common descent. Members of the same nation often recur to the fact that they are descended from the same ancient stock. The belief in such common descent may be greater than the facts warrant: and it is in particular remarkable that members whose ancestors have been very recently transferred to a nation from some neighbouring nation of a different stock, are often enthusiastic believers in their connection with the remote ancestors of those by whom they are surrounded. But the belief in a common descent from those who are perhaps the ancestors of very few of the existing members in a nation, almost always goes side by side with the knowledge of facts which constitute a very strong and very real bond of union. The members of a nation know that the territory which they now occupy or part of it has been for many generations occupied by persons with whom the existing nation may be practically identified, and from whom it inherits historical traditions and the sense of a continuity of national existence. A new nation may indeed come into existence as did the Dutch Republic and the American Union in the 16th and 18th centuries: but in such a case a nation must model itself in some essential respects on the nations already existing, and must be so placed as to be likely to accumulate the traditions and associations necessary to national unity. Otherwise it would differ so considerably from other nations as not to belong at all to the class of states so named.

It would not be difficult to enumerate those states which are generally called nations, and to whose relations with one another the method and phraseology of our science must be adapted. The chief ones among them would be the "great powers" of Europe and the Federal State called the United States of America. A complete enumeration of existing nations and some brief separate discussion of each one of them would be a necessary part of a complete theoretical treatise on International Relations.

As the tie of common descent is the chief

characteristic of a nation, the word nation is often applied to a group of persons similarly descended who do not in fact form a state: and there is an intelligible sense of the word nation in which the Irish at the present time, or the Italians at the time when Italy was a "geographical expression" might be said to form a nation. In the same way some of the very composite states which must be reckoned as nations might be said not to be nations by reason of the obvious want of ethnical unity in their component parts. While admitting the force of such comments we are still at liberty to take that one among the current uses of the word "Nation" which confines it to the description of such communities as are certainly states, and among them to those which are so far national in character as to be generally admitted to stand on the same footing with the great states whose "national" character is undoubted.

The division of states into those which are nations and those which are not is necessarily to some extent an arbitrary division. This fact can hardly be considered as an objection to its employment, since no definite negation is made concerning such states as are not included in the list of states called nations. It is only said that these particular states have so strong a general likeness to one another, and have behaved to so great an extent in the same way and by means of the same organs in their respective historical *rôles*, that it is worth while to consider them as forming a class whose peculiarities may be the subject of theoretical treatment and of a common method and language.

Nothing is denied about other states. The relations of all states with one another have a moral aspect and are the subject of the same great fundamental principles. Among those states which are not considered to be nations, there are many which share a greater or less number of the characteristics of nations and to which therefore any theory applying to nations would more or less nearly apply. It is not necessary to deny of any single state that all which is said of nations would in fact apply to it also. But international relations is the name given to the relations which have in fact existed between a class of states which the similarity of their development, and the language which is employed about them justify us in treating as a class apart among states. We are in no way concerned with the question whether those states which we call nations are the most important states in the world: or whether the national type is that to which all those states which we do not call nations are gradually approaching. Many European reasoners might take an affirmative answer to this question for granted:

but there are probably intelligent persons differing from Europeans in race, colour, religion and customs to whom the possibility of holding such a view would never occur.

## § 2. *Historical Sketch.*

The "nations" of the world then are a particular group of states which we may suppose to have been individually ascertained. But before we could proceed to discuss the relations which arise between nations it would be necessary to do something more than merely to state and apply the tests by which a nation can be known. The use of the word international as an attribute of certain relations implies the acknowledgment that various characteristics are more or less plainly to be perceived in the communities between which those relations exist: and the nature of these characteristics can only be ascertained historically. All states which are either nations by origin or (so to speak) nations by subsequent adoption into the group so named, owe something of their character to the facts surrounding the origin of nations as factors in the world's history, and to the main current of the events which have formed the history of nations from their first appearance down to the present time. An ever-increasing portion of the world's surface has been covered by communities more or less nearly conforming to the national type: and the classification of international relations is intended to apply to relations between those communities, and not to relations to which either or both of the parties belong to the unnationalised communities occupying the remaining portion of the world.

The greater part of the world is now occupied by communities which are not nations, and there is no part of the world which has not been so occupied within historical times. Division into nations is not a necessary attribute of mankind at all times and places: and the necessity of international relations springing up at some time or another among human beings could only be established upon some theory which should embrace the whole chain of causes and effects which constitutes the history of mankind.

It would be necessary in such a historical sketch as is here suggested at least to indicate the particular circumstances in which nations first emerged from a system which was not national in character, and the main current of events which transformed nations from their primitive shape to the highly developed and complicated form which they have now reached. It would require considerable if not unusual audacity to go further and sketch the steps by which in future times the national type may be still further varied and eventually become either universal or obsolete.

The Roman Empire at the time of its greatest vigour and widest extent was not a nation, neither was it a group of nations. Neither the relations of the Empire with states lying beyond its limits nor the relations existing between the several provinces of the Empire resembled the modern relation properly called international by more than a slight analogy. But the Roman Empire was the origin of the nations of the world. They came into existence as it fell asunder, and many of their most prominent characteristics are due to the influence which it exercised over them at the time of its old age and of their youth. Some account of the character of that Empire, of the circumstances of its gradual decay, and of the political ideas which could not fail to occupy the minds of those who witnessed either its feeble shadow at Constantinople, or the attempts to renew and to reinvigorate it in the West, must form a preface to any attempt to give a clear description of the kind of state which is called a nation.

But side by side with the Roman polity which

furnished traditions and ideals to the founders of the national group was another great power which imparted many characteristics to the nascent nations of the world. This was the Christian religion. The student of nations is closely concerned with the nature and history of this religion, with the various sects of those who propagated it in Europe with greater or less success, and especially with the connection of Christianity with the political ideas of Rome, and the action and reaction of these two forces on each other.

At the time then when Europe was occupied by a number of tribes and states from which those nations who have been spoken of as the kernel of the national system were slowly to emerge, there were three great forces at work: the character of the independent races which had surrounded the Roman Empire and occupied its territory, the ideas and traditions of the Roman Empire and the Christian religion. Other influences infinite in number and complexity were also in existence: but it would be impossible to have anything like a complete idea of what sort of states those which we call nations are, without having to some extent studied at least these three great elements of European activity.

From a very early period of European history,

the two forces of imperial unity and of national independence have been at work side by side. Some parts of Europe have been remarkable for the rapid development of the latter, some for the prolonged vitality of the former force. But on the whole the history of Europe has been that of the development of national independence at the expense of imperial unity. The decisive crisis was passed at the Reformation, when the possibility of the complete independence of some at least of the nations in their religious capacity took the place of a general acknowledgment that Europe was one at all events for religious purposes. The early history of the German Empire and of the Papacy is that of the fluctuations in the vitality and vigour of that spirit of unity whose complete triumph or survival would have so much modified the character of international relations. The real suzerainty of some of the emperors over European kings and the way in which popes like Innocent III exercised a practical superintendence over the conduct of kings and the relations of kingdoms, illustrate the results which the realisation of the unity of Europe might have produced. The European Crusades and the idea of a common resistance to Mahometan and other eastern invaders are further illustrations of these results. Though the opposite tendency has proved the stronger, these facts and the feelings which they have left behind them must be borne in mind in realising the character of nations as contrasted with other kinds of political communities.

Besides the original elements of national life, and the great principle at whose expense, but also under whose powerful influence, the nations of Europe have grown up, we must take into account some of the special circumstances which gave some important characteristics to European nations at their first appearance. The complicated system of society called Feudalism not only played its part in the struggle between national independence and imperial unity, but also bequeathed characteristics to the nations of Europe which had important effects on the character of international relations. It would be impossible to understand the history of international relations without some knowledge of the way in which a mediæval king was looked on as the proprietor of the territory ruled by him and the representative of his subjects: down to a very recent time it was more usual to look upon a man as the subject and therefore almost as the property of a particular prince than as the member of an independent community: and any portion of land would be more naturally spoken of as belonging to a sovereign than as being the home of a nation. On the whole the feudal system was more adapted to that theory of European unity which did not survive, but of which there were very numerous examples a century ago and of which there are still some illustrations: but although feudalism was opposed to that one of the conflicting principles which was eventually successful, it very considerably modified the workings of that principle.

But it would not be enough to indicate the leading characteristics of the process by which the nations of Europe—a class of states till that time without precedent in the history of political institutions—grew into existence among the *débris* of the Roman Empire. It is about 400 years since it first became apparent that the mediæval scheme of European politics had failed, and that the principle of the unity of Christendom had definitely yielded to the principle of separate nations, though the power of the Papacy and the authority of the German Empire still interfered greatly with the realisation of the new ideal. Europe was in 1500 divided into nations sufficiently similar to the nations of to-day to fall naturally into the same group of political communities. Since that time there have been several attempts by powerful individuals to restore European unity and to crush national independence. But on the whole the nations of the western world have become stronger and have acquired a more distinct individuality. The history of Germany, Italy and Greece in the present century strongly exemplifies the persistence and developments of the national type. But during the same period momentous changes have taken place which have modified the idea called up in our minds by the use of the word nation and which have introduced new classes of international relations. That is to say that there are new kinds of relations whose existence to a greater or less extent may be presumed between any states which have justified their being reckoned as members of the class called nations. The most important of these great events is the discovery and colonisation of a new continent and of other great tracts of land. New kinds of national ambition, new causes of international quarrels, new modes of thought, and a new type of nations—the imperial nation under whose rule dependencies or free colonies are combined into an empire—have come into existence.

The relations existing between nations and between them and other states more or less nearly conforming to the national type, became far more numerous and complex with the great increase in scientific knowledge and in commercial enterprise which has been characteristic of the last four centuries: and the new elements of national life took their place side by side with those which were inherited from the Teutonic tribes or from the Romans of the Empire, or which had come into existence owing to the doctrines of feudalism. A new class of international relations grew up in later times from the desire on the part of similarly situated classes in different nations for a more democratic form of government. The rebellion of the Netherlands, the political changes in England in the seventeenth century, the revolt of the American Colonies, and the French Revolution are instances of events in national life which could not fail to modify the character of nations and to give rise to a new class of international relations. A further development of the same kind, attended by similar results, is to be found in the economic theories and especially the schemes of socialism advocated in various nations at the present time.

The old feudal idea that a king was a proprietor who had accumulated a large family estate and who would act naturally in trying to add yet further to it, did much to give their character to early European wars: and from this class of wars was developed the idea of the Balance of Power, and the leagues formed from time to time for its preservation. The connection of Elizabeth with the Netherlands, or of the United States with Revolutionary France, and the proceedings of the Holy Alliance and of those who were opposed to it, illustrate the kind of international relations which originated in the frequent appearance in nations of a party determined to resist by force either arbitrary power on the one hand or popular sedition on the other. International leagues for the promotion of the interests of the labouring classes, and those for the abolition of all social and political institutions, illustrate different effects upon international relations of more recent kinds of opinions.

When the American colonies, first of England and afterwards of Spain, attained independence, new states came into existence which sufficiently resembled the European type to be reckoned as nations, and to hold such intercourse with the old nations as made their relations with them amenable to the same scientific arrangement and phraseology. Some Asiatic communities have shown more or less desire and aptitude for a similar kind of intercourse. It is possible that some day all the known communities of the world may so nearly resemble the same type that all relations between them will be fitly described as international. If this should happen it will be the result of the actual course of European political history and of the tendency of non-European communities to imitate those nations which have been directly affected by that history. If such a homogeneous condition of mankind should happen to be brought about, it may subsequently happen to disappear through similar historical agencies: and a new type or new types of communities may occupy the attention of mankind. Meanwhile we are immediately concerned with the national type such as circumstances have made it and in those places to which it has in fact been extended.

### § 3. *The Representation of Nations by Governments.*

Having ascertained which among existing states are those called nations, and what the general features of the historical career of that group of states have been, we have to consider what are the principal national institutions which will be brought into contact with one another so as to give rise to international relations. A great many elements of national life which would be very important if we were discussing political institutions generally, are of a subordinate interest in such an inquiry as this. Those things which may be of the highest importance to individuals as members of any nation, may have no prominence at all in the picture of the same individuals and their institutions as it is presented to members of another nation: in the same way a man may lead an active and busy life as a public servant or in any other capacity which brings him constantly into contact with the political machinery of his own country, and may yet seldom or never have his attention drawn to the international aspect of the nation, or to those characteristics in it which are the most important in the eyes of a foreigner.

The chief principle of international relations is that for all international purposes a nation is completely represented by its government. This is obviously true with respect to that large and important part of international relations which demonstrably consists of relations between one government and another. But it is also true of all really international relations. A member of one nation who is at the moment in any sort of relation with members of another nation, is looked on by them for some purposes as if he were not a foreigner at all: he is also looked on as a person who is considered more or less likely to display the temper, demeanour and habits supposed to be characteristic of his compatriots: but so far as any general rules can be laid down about the peculiarities of relations entered into with such a foreigner, so far that is as those relations can be distinctly and intelligibly described as international, he is to be considered as a person who is represented and can be supported by a known government having a corporate existence, recognised organs for intercourse with other governments, and a character and history which are to some extent matter of public notoriety. Nothing definite can be laid down in general terms about the character of transactions entered into by Frenchmen visiting England with Englishmen there resident, except in so far as such relations can be the subject either of intercourse between the two governments or of rules and systems laid down by the one, and ascertainable by the other. When an Englishman speaks of a Frenchman the use of the word may call up in his own mind and that of his hearers no other idea than that of a man connected with a particular part of the world and a particular set of historical facts, and having his place in a state of society and under a legal and administrative system with which different Englishmen may happen to be more or less acquainted. But in this case the use of the word French is not international: if it have any international sense it must bring up in the minds of those who use it, some idea of the French government, either as capable of entering into relations with their own government and through it with them, or as the maker and enforcer of laws by which they may be affected. All the international relations of this country must necessarily be either relations into which the English government enters with the government of another nation: or relations between English individuals and foreign governments: or relations between the English government and foreign individuals: or relations between English and foreign individuals. And the fact now insisted on amounts to this: that with regard to all the above classes of relations in which any mention is made of individuals, such relations only are truly international as have some connection with the governments by which those individuals can be represented.

It will then be desirable before proceeding to consider the several classes of international relations to look at some of the characteristics which are common to the group of governments which exist, one of them representing the individuals who compose each of the nations now existing.

The word government is the most convenient one to employ, because it is in fact the one generally used, for the purpose of designating collectively the body of persons who in fact conduct a part of the internal business of every nation, and who are entrusted with the control of its diplomatic relations and the management of its foreign affairs.

A "government" in the modern sense of the term is not synonymous with the expression "sovereign" or "sovereign body" in the science of jurisprudence or politics[1]. In a literally monarchical state, where the sovereign is an autocratic individual, the government would consist of a group of ministers, who were entrusted by the monarch with the management of the various departments of public affairs and who were directly responsible to their master. In such a state (if such a one is really possible or even conceivable) the actual force supporting legislation, and indirectly such institutions and arrangements as depend on legislation, would be the monarch's will: "the government" would be an intelligible name for the group of officials to whom the monarch must leave a considerable latitude in the interpretation and application of his wishes, if the internal administration of the country, or its diplomatic relations were at all numerous and complicated, and if their stability was thought desirable. In a nation where the sovereign body was an

[1] In accordance with common usage however, and to avoid the constant use of the phrase "sovereign body" the word government is often used in this essay as a synonym for "sovereign body" when the making of laws is being discussed.

assembly representative of all the sane and adult population, the government would in the same way be persons appointed by them, responsible to them, and temporarily armed with their full authority, for the purpose of conducting public affairs. In actual nations whose constitution more or less nearly approximates to that now suggested, the government generally includes some executive official, hereditary or elected, who is not a member of the representative assembly. Its chief members are in many nations, members of that assembly and those upon whom it has informally conferred preëminence. In other nations the principal members of the government are excluded from the representative assembly. There are different kinds of machinery for bringing the wishes of electors, more or less in connection with the personal predilections of individuals distinguished by birth or otherwise, to bear on the nomination of the chief members of the government. Subordinate members of the government who are almost always excluded from the representative assembly, may be appointed either by its principal members or by those who appointed them.

Every existing nation possesses a constitution which comes somewhere between absolute monarchy and absolute democracy: and the variety among these constitutions is sufficiently great to make the characteristics which are common to all national governments rather few in number. The general notion of these characteristics can be gathered from the above summary of the relation between "government" and the actual "sovereign" or "sovereign body" possessing the force by which laws are sanctioned.

The actual constitution of a nation, or the manner in which the sovereign power is therein owned and exercised is a matter which does not particularly concern other nations. What does concern them is that there should be a recognisable corporation consisting of officials entrusted by the sovereign body, of whatever kind that body may be, with the duty of representing for the time being the nation and any individual belonging to it whether in an active or a passive capacity, and having control of the national resources for the purpose of so doing.

There is one question of political science which is exceedingly important in connection with our present topic, but of which only a very slight mention can be made here. That is the question of the distinction between the various kinds of federal and confederate governments. This is in fact a question which lies at the bottom of all political theory. No government can be devised which can superintend even to the slightest extent every kind of public business in the state. Every government contents itself with attending to some parts of public affairs and leaving others to be dealt with by practically independent local corporations. Therefore every nation may be looked upon as a community consisting of a number of corporations which manage some of their affairs independently, but which submit to the general control of a common governing body to whom they also entrust the direct superintendence of other parts of their affairs. But a federal state is nothing but a community of this kind where the independent corporations are unusually large and the affairs left to the common government are unusually few.

Now in most nations which may properly be called federal the duty of entering into relations with other nations, whether on behalf of individuals or in any other way, is one of those classes of affairs which is not left to the state or provincial governments, but belongs solely to the imperial or common government. But in some federations, and in composite empires where much freedom of self-government is allowed to parts of the empire, and in those nations which are beyond the line separating the federal state (*bundesstat*) from the confederation or permanent alliance of states (*statenbund*), there may be some purposes for which the subordinate governments are capable of entering into foreign relations and of representing the individuals subject to them in transactions with other governments. Cases of this amount of independence and its various degrees must be collected by the observation of existing institutions and of constitutional provisions on the subject.

### § 4. *Laws of International Import.*

The existence and the circumstances of a nation may become interesting to any other nation in as many different ways as there are phases of national activity. The political development, the commercial enterprise, the progress or retrogression in civilisation, the growth of science or literature in one nation may act more or less directly on the corporate life of another nation. But there is one department of national activity in which it is particularly likely that international relations will have their origin. Every nation is not only a community for the furtherance of commercial, agricultural, artistic, literary and other kinds of activity: but also and especially a community for the enactment and enforcement of laws. Among the kinds of international relations to which the career of civilised mankind has given rise, many have their origin in legislation: and of these no class is more important and more distinct than that which is due to the effect of the laws made and enforced by one nation upon the individuals belonging to another nation.

In order to form a true idea of this class of international relations it will be necessary, before going at all into detail, to consider briefly what is the nature, origin and effect of laws in general.

In every nation the sovereign power resides in some determinate body to whom the whole nation is in the habit of rendering obedience. Legislative organs are provided by which the sovereign body, or those to whom the authority of that body is periodically entrusted, subject to a more or less definite intermediate control, can enact laws to be observed by all members of the nation. Judicial organs are provided by which the laws so enacted can be expounded and applied. A more or less elaborate branch of the administrative organisation of the nation is so contrived as to put the force wielded by the government practically at the disposal of the magistrates who apply the law to actual quarrels and misdeeds. A law, in its simplest form, is a command on behalf of the state, to persons subject to the jurisdiction of the legislature, to do or abstain from doing a specified class of actions, under pain of suffering a specified evil at the hands of the officers of the government. The plainest instance of this is a rule of criminal law by which the members of a nation are laid under a duty to abstain from a particular kind of conduct and a definite sanction is provided to prevent or to punish any violation of that duty. The same elements can be discovered in other laws which are less direct illustrations of the true nature of a law. In laws directing the observance of particular kinds of contracts, and in laws giving a remedy to individuals who suffer particular kinds of wrongs, a duty is laid upon individuals in their relations with other individuals, and such arrangements are more or less distinctly made for the enunciation and enforcement of these duties in particular cases as will, in the last resort, if authoritative threats prove useless, lead to the forcible intervention of state officials to see that the thing forbidden is not done or that the stipulated reparation is made.

These laws, creating rights and duties under the direct protection of the government, are often made and can most conveniently be made by legislation or the distinct and formal orders of the acknowledged legislature. They can also be made by the tacit acknowledgment of rules said to be founded on ancient custom, and enforced by the tribunals which are the judicial organs of the sovereign body. A rule which is habitually applied by such tribunals, and in the application of which they are habitually supported by the government, may possess all the characteristics of a law, though the legislature has not precisely formulated it and though its origin may be plainly traced to the decision of a particular judicial officer. We must not expect always to be able to find the deliberate expression by the legislature of a particular rule: we must sometimes infer their tacit acceptance of it from the fact that it has not been disowned and that the executive authority has been put at the disposal of the tribunals for its enforcement.

In every nation, then, laws are made, to which the legislative organs of the sovereign body have openly or tacitly expressed their assent, and which owe their legal character to the fact that the executive organs of the sovereign body assist their enforcement if necessary by physical constraint of those who have offended or are likely to offend against the laws. Our object will be to see, in a general way, how the existence of such laws can affect the existing relations or can give rise to new relations between one nation and another.

A law which is made by the legislature of one country can in no case be necessarily a matter of absolute and permanent indifference to any other nation. Most laws are made for the regulation of the conduct of persons who are subject to the jurisdiction of the courts of the legislating country. The jurisdiction of particular courts is defined with more or less accuracy by the legislature: and the jurisdiction of a particular court is generally confined to persons within the territory of the country to which it belongs or to some subdivision of such persons. But members of one nation must often find themselves within the territory of another nation. During their sojourn there they are subject to the jurisdiction of its courts. They will be practically affected by the laws of that country, whether by the juridical character attached to the acts which they do, or by the interpretation given to the contracts which they make.

Apart from the question of the international aspect of laws in general and especially of the laws conferring a jurisdiction for particular purposes upon special courts, there are some laws of which the international aspect is obviously and avowedly important. There are firstly laws regulating the conduct of the members of a nation or of the government itself, towards foreigners: secondly, laws by which a government directly regulates the conduct of foreigners.

In the following sections an attempt is made

to indicate the principal kinds of legislation which would fall into each of the above-mentioned classes. There are many kinds of laws directly relating to foreigners which are administered in times of peace: at such times the mutual forbearance and recognition of one another's independence which are characteristic of nations in their normal relation, render unlikely any but a very limited indulgence in legislation for foreigners outside the territory of the legislating nation. But some of the laws relating to the relation of war, and especially those which have reference to the relations between belligerents and neutrals, are best explained as examples of legislation by the government of one nation for the individuals belonging to another.

The general function of municipal law (to borrow Blackstone's name for the public law of separate states) with regard to international relations and international morality is exceedingly important. The nations of the world are actuated by all kinds of ambitions and sentiments, they are severe critics of the conduct of their neighbours, they can behave well and they can behave badly. Under all the conflicting motives of prudence, benevolence, ambition or jealousy which beset a particular problem of international ethics, a nation has to decide how to act without any external compulsory motives except the fear of the resentment and possibly the forcible restraint and retaliation of its neighbours. There is no formal and efficient international sanction. Morality however is not entirely dependent on formal and efficient law: and as there are many motives which would incline enlightened men to observe regular rules in their mutual intercourse, although there were no legal sanction to compel them to do so, so statesmen are actuated by a desire that their own and other nations should behave to one another with the uniformity and moderation which are expected from men subject to law. Statesmen have therefore often declared their intention to abide by the "law of nations" and called upon the governments of other nations to do the same: and solemn promises have been made by treaty to observe specified rules of international intercourse, whether those rules are declared to be a part of the law of nations or are recommended as a salutary deviation from them. But the "law of nations" is only a conventional name for a kind of morality of which the sanctions do not possess that formal and certain character essential to Law proper, but rather resemble the sanctions attaching to ordinary morality unprotected by law: and the promises made by treaty differ in the same way from contracts or promises protected by law in communities subject to law. It therefore seems that some further guarantee is desirable for statesmen who wish to bind themselves and their successors to follow the dictates of international law. Such a farther guarantee, though not an international sanction, is obtained by means of municipal law. There are many ways in which the regular tribunals of a nation can give effect to a particular view of a question of international morality. The opinion of a particular legislature on the bearing of "the law of nations" can be put into the shape of distinct legislation. The promises made by treaties can in the same way be guaranteed by explicit legislation. This is generally done in cases of much complication, and in all cases the courts of a nation will probably take judicial notice of a treaty, should occasion arise.

The importance of this use of municipal law for international purposes is that it affords a sanction applying practically and effectively to individuals, and that it gives precision to the course pursued by one government upon matters which may excite the interest and even the interference of another government. Much of the most important part of international morality relates to the conduct of governments alone, and with regard to this municipal law has no application: but the assistance of municipal law is available and desirable wherever international morality is concerned with the conduct or the treatment of individuals.

## § 5. *Peace.*

### A. *General Characteristics.*

States are naturally self-sufficient and independent, and if we were concerned with states in general and with the history of the world, we might perhaps arrive at the conclusion that the normal international relation was that of habitual indifference tempered by jealous distrust and frequent violence. But we have to deal only with that particular class of states to which we have restricted the use of the name nation, and we may say of them that they are by no means altogether indifferent to one another; since the attention of each is constantly occupied with the department of national activity consisting in the superintendence of foreign affairs: that unrestrained international violence and rapacity are almost unknown, the definite and regulated forms of violence collectively called War having taken their place: and that the normal relation subsisting among them is that of Peace.

We must set out then by considering the

elements of the condition called Peace and the general attributes of nations living together in that condition. The principal characteristics of this condition consist in the mutual forbearances which it implies. Nations at peace with one another do not consider themselves called upon to interfere, except in cases of extreme gravity, when the administration of the laws of one nation affects in any way the individuals belonging to another. The government of a nation takes a benevolent interest in its subjects wherever they may be, but as a general rule it does not in any way object to the inconveniences to which they may be submitted by the effects of their temporary subjection to the jurisdiction of civil and criminal courts differently constituted and administering a different law from those of their own country. The applications of its sovereign power which a government makes with impunity to the persons of all who come within its territory are also suffered to go unchallenged to a more or less limited extent with regard to persons on board ships which belong to it, and to persons on board foreign ships in specified portions of the sea. This extensive sufferance by all nations of the exercise of foreign authority by foreign governments over their own subjects is the strongest instance of the acknowledgment of the sovereignty of one government by another. With respect to the way in which a government treats its own territory and its own subjects the indulgence of foreign governments naturally goes much further, and is never likely to give place to remonstrance or interference except in very extreme cases.

But while on the one hand we note the respect for the independence of one nation shown by another, we must on the other hand observe the consideration and hospitality shown by one nation to individuals of another. Among nations a traveller does not come into a foreign land at his own risk but is habitually treated like an inhabitant of the country as far as the general protection and conveniences afforded by the government are concerned. Since nations have existed there have been many kinds of modifications in and exceptions to this general hospitality, and there still exist various methods of making a foreigner feel that he is to some extent an object of suspicion and liable to be treated differently from those by whom he is surrounded. But on the whole a foreigner in times of peace may safely reckon on being placed on nearly the same footing as the natives of the country where he is. Various devices have been made by different governments for the complete absorption of individuals who have been subjects of one government, into the community which is subject to another. This ordinary international hospitality is extended in some cases to the bestowal of exceptional privileges. Thus a travelling king or prince, or an ex-sovereign sojourning in a foreign land, is likely to find himself held to enjoy immunity from some kinds of jurisdiction; it is for instance possible that a government would even at the present day abstain from prosecuting a travelling ex-Queen who had her prime minister stabbed in her private residence: though it would be unwise to try an experiment so likely to bring the offender within the extreme cases which must form exceptions to any practice of international hospitality. Similar privileges have been allowed in various degrees to ambassadors and to the less important representatives of foreign states. Foreign ships of war and foreign merchant ships which happen to be in the harbour of a nation enjoy various degrees of immunity from the authority of the government.

Under the influence of these two national habits, respect for one another's independence, and mutual hospitality to individuals, the various relations which make up the condition of peace have greatly increased in number and importance. There are innumerable species of commercial relations between the individuals of different nations: governments borrow money from foreigners; individuals contract to work for hire for foreign governments: and every kind of contractual relation springs up between members of different nations. These various kinds of international intercourse cannot exist without the necessity for direct intercourse between the several governments. This direct intercourse is further necessitated by the conflicting interests of existing nations as to the arrangements which nations may separately make with one another, and as to the general foreign policy which a particular nation may pursue. Accordingly organs for such direct influence are provided. Governments address one another through the mouths of their agents or by the publication of state papers, and there is a free interchange of national opinion on events of international importance. At great crises the machinery of Congresses can be employed. Some instances may be given of the topics which international Congresses have discussed, and upon which they have pronounced decisions of a more or less detailed and practical character. They have asserted the sovereign rights of dynasties, and determined the boundaries of contiguous territories: they have given to particular nations various degrees of authority over places formerly subject to other nations: they have demanded the toleration of classes of subjects by sovereigns otherwise likely to persecute them: they have made declarations of what they consider to be right and praiseworthy conduct for nations to pursue under many kinds of circumstances: they have given their authority to arrangements for the navigation of specified rivers and inland seas: and they have acted as arbitrators in particular emergencies.

Besides the Congresses where several nations have jointly discussed international affairs and have arrived at conclusions more or less directly affecting them, there are those more private and personal discussions of two or more nations with one another which result in the formation of treaties. A congress of a considerable number of nations may make a treaty, though it need not necessarily do so; but the arrangement to which the name treaty is naturally applied is one to which the representatives of two or three nations have agreed each on behalf of their own nation.

A treaty between two nations is a definite and formal declaration that each of the nations which are parties to it will adopt towards the other a particular line of conduct therein set forth, or will permit the other to act in a specified way. A nation may agree by treaty either to admit or actively to support the right of a particular family to rule over another nation: to allow or actively to assist another nation to annex or absorb territory previously independent or subject to another government: to give upon stipulated conditions certain commercial privileges to the members of another nation: to adopt certain methods of warfare in any future dispute with another nation, or to allow to its members certain privileges and immunities if they should be in a position of neutrals when the nation so agreeing is at war. Treaties may be made for the purpose of enunciating the terms upon which a victorious nation consents to make peace with a conquered nation: or for the establishment between nations which have common interests of an alliance which may be of any degree of closeness between that of a permanent confederacy and that of common but independent exertions for the attainment of a specified object.

The common comparison of a treaty to a contract between individuals is likely to mislead because of the great differences due to the absence of positive law or anything nearly resembling it to enforce the agreement[1]. In fact a treaty is no

[1] It has however been already explained that though there is no law by which governments are compelled to keep treaties

more than a solemn statement by the representatives of two nations of the present intention of those nations to do that which they agree to do. Nations are necessarily inclined by moral motives to observe the promises thus made: the breach of a treaty by one party will almost necessarily excite indignation in the other party or parties to it, and may excite indignation in nations not parties to it in a degree depending on the surrounding circumstances of the case. An agreement into which a nation enters under the fear of instant violence if it refuses, or an agreement to do things which subsequently appear to be incompatible with the national welfare to an extent which neither party had expected at the time of making the treaty, may be violated without incurring great indignation on the part of nations in general. Experience shows that in a time of general war and great international animosities promises made by treaty are often violated recklessly, and the fact of their being so violated attracts slight attention and does not produce the international consequences which follow such conduct in normal times.

### B. *Laws of International Import.*

There is no class of laws of which it can be

there may be laws by which governments compel individuals to act in accordance with their provisions.

certainly said that they will under no circumstances possess international import or give rise to international relations. Upon any matter which is made the subject of legislation a legislature might directly or tacitly lay down rules so affecting an individual habitually subject to a foreign government, as to lead to remonstrances on the part of that government. A short time ago the criminal responsibility incurred by an English subject who took upon himself public functions in Germany led to diplomatic intercourse on the subject between the two governments: and more recently still we have heard something of the probability of pressure being brought to bear on the English by the American government on account of the alleged hardships inflicted on an American subject by the rules of English criminal procedure.

But while every part of the legal system of a nation may have an effect upon foreign individuals, and through them upon international relations proper, there are some kinds of laws which are specially likely to affect foreigners.

Legislation for the protection of native industry and many kinds of laws incidental to the regulation of commerce: laws about the interpretation of bills of exchange: laws about the protection given to inventors, to authors of books or works of art, and to tradesmen or manufacturers who have adopted a particular trade-mark: laws relating to the validity of marriage: laws directing particular rules of navigation to be observed at sea, prohibiting various offences under the name of smuggling, regulating the right of fishing in specified places, or dealing with the treatment of wrecks and the payment of salvage: laws giving practical sanctions to international arrangements about railways, telegraphs, or the carriage of letters: laws creating rights or duties in connection with the use of passports by travellers: laws making rules, or empowering corporations to make them, about the navigation of rivers: and many other classes of laws which might be mentioned are instances of municipal laws more than usually likely to affect the comfort and well-being of individuals belonging to other nations, and therefore likely from time to time to attract the attention of the governments by whom those individuals are represented. Statutes dealing with some of the above topics necessarily contain many sections having direct reference to foreigners and to acts done in foreign countries.

In addition to laws which for one reason or another are likely to affect foreigners as well as the subjects of the legislating government, there are some in which foreign governments themselves are directly interested and which are especially made for their convenience.

The question of the naturalisation of foreign individuals is one that is very important to foreign governments: the exact manner in which citizenship in a nation can be obtained by forms or ceremonies or is acquired by birth, as well as the circumstances (if any) in which it is held to come to an end, have been the subject of regular legislation in all nations, and the sanctions of municipal law are employed to enforce the various systems existing in different parts of the world. The introduction of formal legislation on this subject has been a great boon to nations: for when different nations applied different principles to the question, in virtue of an indefinite common law, alleged to be borrowed from a still more indefinite "law of nations," international disputes about questions of citizenship were more likely to arise and less likely to be easily and finally settled. Legal provisions are in the same way distinctly and definitely, though differently, made by different nations as to the facts which imply a particular nationality in a ship.

Another topic as to which nations have agreed on the desirability of embodying their intentions in regular municipal laws is that of extradition. Every nation is reluctant to acquiesce in the impunity of a member who has offended against its criminal law and who has subsequently escaped to foreign territory: at the same time no nation is willing to give up any one accused of any crime without question or delay to a foreign government who asserts that he has offended against its criminal law, nor to give up those whose criminality and allegiance are clearly proved except in the cases where the criminal nature of the act is universally admitted. The effect of these conflicting sentiments upon the facts of a particular case is a question of international morality or, as statesmen prefer to say, of "international law": and it has often happened, in the absence of previous agreements or of municipal law, that the views of two governments as to the dictates of morality have differed. Many nations have now promised one another by treaty to effect the extradition of criminals, in the case of specified crimes, and under specified conditions. Such treaties are protected by elaborate municipal legislation respecting the procedure to be observed in cases where extradition is demanded: and the existence of such treaties and such laws minimises the evil effects of the doubts surrounding the moral problem.

But the direct interest of a government in offenders situated in foreign territory is not confined to its own escaped criminals: it is also concerned with those who either publish abuse of it or hatch crimes of violence against it in a foreign land. This natural feeling is opposed, at least as strongly as in the case of extradition, by the natural unwillingness of governments to acquiesce in interference or dictation from without. Here too however a compromise between the conflicting sentiments is possible, and it will be all the more satisfactory if it has the precision and effectiveness derived from municipal legislation. Two examples of such laws may be given, one from the common law and one from the statute-book of our own country. They will show in what form laws affecting this particular kind of international relations can be made. Each of them reminds us of a dispute between England and France arising in the conflict of the two sentiments mentioned above and very nearly resulting in war between the two countries. In the case of Peltier, who published violent abuse of Napoleon during the Peace of Amiens in 1802, Lord Ellenborough, after referring to some earlier cases of the same kind, said, "I lay it down as the law that any "publication which tends to disgrace, revile and "defame persons of considerable situations of "power and dignity in foreign countries, may be "taken to be and may be treated as a (criminal) "libel; and particularly where it has a tendency "to interrupt the amity and peace between the "two countries[1]." On the second of the topics under discussion, The Criminal Law Consolidation Acts contain provisions for the punishment of any person conspiring to murder, or soliciting, encouraging, persuading, endeavouring to persuade, or proposing to any person to murder a person not a subject of the Queen, and not within the Queen's dominions[2]. As in the case of extradition, such laws as these do not entirely obviate international difficulties founded on the difficulties surrounding international morality: but their existence and their probable practical efficiency, simplify particular controversies.

Another subject on which the agency of law is beneficially employed in giving precision to international relations, is the position of ambassadors and consuls and the privileges and immunities allowed to them. In this country no definite legislative enactment gives a comprehensive statement of the rights and privileges of foreign ambassadors: but their freedom and that of their registered servants (unless they are traders) from arrest and other process, are practically guaranteed by statute (7 Anne, c. 12).

[1] Folkard's *Starkie on Libel*, 670.
[2] Stephen's *Digest of the Criminal Law*, p. 154.

Ambassadors' privileges in respect of criminal legislation, and the necessary limitations upon these privileges in extreme cases, form part of the common law (i.e. the view of English judges as to the bearing of the law of nations), and the fewness of the cases which have actually occurred makes it difficult to ascertain exactly what the provisions of the common law are.

There is no reason why the whole question of the *status* of foreign ambassadors together with that of foreign consuls, who are in many cases already the subject of consular conventions between different governments, should not in every country be the subject of full and explicit legal provisions, such as would make perfectly plain such differences as exist in the views held by different governments as to the exact effect of morality and expediency upon the matter. In addition to legislation about the ambassadors and other diplomatic agents and the consuls of foreign powers, there is also of necessity some legislation, by statute or by decided cases, about the same officers when sent by the legislative power to foreign countries. In the case of ambassadors, &c., such legislation is hardly likely to go beyond settling how they are to be appointed and paid: but as regards consuls the nature of their duties and jurisdiction has often been and must be the subject of detailed legislation by the power whom they represent.

Besides the various kinds of substantive law which are specially likely to affect foreigners, there are various laws defining the jurisdiction of particular courts whose provisions have great international importance. Express or tacit legislation determines in every nation the territorial limits of jurisdiction, and settles what persons shall have access to particular courts and to what extent remedies shall be given in respect of acts done in foreign territory, or regard shall be had to the provisions of foreign laws. Wherever disabilities have been attached or are still attached to aliens in the country of their temporary residence, they are to some extent in the form of legal restraints upon their access to civil courts.

The limits of territorial jurisdiction are a very proper subject for legislation: the difficulties surrounding the question of international morality are very great. All nations are ready to allow the extension of the jurisdiction of a government over the whole of the territory subject to it; but difficulties have arisen about the question of jurisdiction at sea. Persons on board a merchant ship within a short distance of a foreign coast, or persons on board a ship of war in a foreign harbour, may be said according to one view or another of international morality and convenience to be in the jurisdiction of the sovereign to whom they are ordinarily subject, or of the sovereign to whose territory they have nearly approached. The weight of the conflicting arguments will appear different to different governments, and each will practically adopt a compromise, giving to itself a control for some purposes over a merchant ship within a specified distance of its coast, and allowing to ships of war within its harbours an immunity from local jurisdiction subject to such limitations in extreme cases as appear to it to be desirable. The Territorial Waters Act of 1878 is an example of this kind of legislation. It professes to be merely declaratory of the Law of Nations, that is of the bearing of international law, on the subject of criminal jurisdiction in territorial waters, and to provide machinery by which that jurisdiction shall be exercised: but it is in effect an enactment of the legislature deciding that such jurisdiction shall extend as far as is necessary for the protection and safety of the Queen's dominions, that is at least to the extent of one marine league from the English coast, and farther if there is any justification for such further extension in "international law." The real nature of this enactment is shown by the fact that the law which it professes to declare was a direct reversal of the law laid down by the majority of the judges in the case of the *Franconia*. In fact an alteration was made in the law of territorial jurisdiction of England by a regular legislative enactment. There is no reason why the legislatures of all nations should not exactly and explicitly lay down the extent to which they intend to exercise such jurisdiction, as well as the immunity which they will allow to foreign ships of war whether in their territorial waters or in their harbours. If a dispute arose for decision upon any of these questions it would have to be decided somehow, and the decision would have the regular sanctions attaching to the decisions of a tribunal authorised by a sovereign government. In other words there is necessarily in every nation law, affirming or denying the extension of the whole or parts of the nation's jurisdiction to any given place; and where there is such law it is capable of distinct legislative expression. If the laws of different nations be found so to conflict as to lead to practical inconvenience, that is a matter for diplomatic discussion between their governments.

Criminal jurisdiction must be conferred by every government upon some one or more of its courts with respect to acts done on board its own ships (if it has any) upon the "high seas," where no regular territorial jurisdiction exists. In connection with this kind of jurisdiction occurs the principal example of anything like criminal law, enacted by each government for all persons in whatever place they may be at the time of doing the criminal act. This example is that of "piracy by the law of nations." This crime is one which our own legislature has frequently had occasion to mention but which it has not thought it necessary to define. It may be said, without any pretension to great accuracy, that piracy is the doing or manifest intent to do acts of violence or robbery in a place where there is no regular national jurisdiction, by those who have the control and management of a ship, under circumstances which do not make the government of any nation responsible for the acts done. Piracy is said to be contrary to the "law of nations": and it cannot be denied that it ought to be condemned and if possible punished upon every ground of morality and expediency. But any punishment inflicted upon pirates is inflicted by particular nations and in virtue of municipal laws. It is a settled part of the law of England that persons belonging to any nation who have committed piracy at sea are amenable to the criminal jurisdiction of the Admiral[1], now exercised by the

[1] Stephen's *History of the Criminal Law*, II. 27. See also pages 18—22.

High Court, and there are various judicial dicta giving definitions of piracy by the law of nations, which are to some extent limited owing to the circumstances of the particular cases, but which all point to some variation of the crime described above. The readiness of the English common law to give effect to a wider definition of piracy may be inferred from the mention of piracy as an acknowledged and well-understood pursuit in other statutes referring to British subjects only. The language of some of these statutes "seems to "imply that a pirate is a known class of persons "like a soldier or sailor, and that a man may be a "pirate though he has never robbed, as he may be "a soldier though he has never fought[1]."

The general view of piracy by the governments of existing nations seems to be that it is a crime which is best punishable by those who detect the offenders, and no government authorising the enforcement of a law against piracy is likely to be troubled by complaints of another government whose subject an individual pirate may prove himself to be. The laws of most nations say with more or less distinctness, and those of all might say with perfect distinctness, and with a full definition of the acts or evidence of intention constituting piracy, "All men, of whatever nation-

[1] Stephen's *Digest of the Criminal Law*, p. 73, n.

"ality or allegiance, are forbidden to commit acts "of piracy, under specified penalties." This would be municipal law in each country, subject to municipal sanctions, and it might be beneficially enforced although the exact definition of the crime and the machinery for punishing it might differ in different countries.

It has been a matter of judicial discussion in this country whether the law authorises the punishment of acts of slave-trading done upon the high seas by persons not subjects of the Queen, and the decision has on the whole been that it does not. The severe laws made by many nations against slave-trading have however possessed great international importance. The great obstacle to enacting a general law against acts of slave-trading is that the carrying out of such a law involves the search by armed ships of foreign ships in time of peace: if such a search is not allowed, any ship engaged in the slave-trade can protect itself by carrying the flag of a nation at peace with the nation which is hostile to the slave-trade.

On the whole it has not been found convenient to extend the elaborate regulations of the criminal law on the subject beyond the limits of the ordinary jurisdiction: and it is usual to put down the trade as carried on by foreigners by what are practically acts of war, although it is not generally the will or the interest of foreign governments so to regard them, and by means of treaties between the powers who especially desire the discontinuance of this traffic. Such treaties contain elaborate provisions as to the way in which ships of the nations who are parties to the treaty shall be dealt with when there is a suspicion that they are breaking the law of their own nation with regard to the slave-trade. The international aspect of laws against the slave-trade may be thus summed up; some nations forbid their own subjects by law to engage in this trade, and others do not: many of the nations which do forbid it have promised each other by treaty to coöperate in a specified manner in the execution of their laws: they have further promised in the same way to coöperate in forcibly restraining the subjects of other nations from engaging in the trade. The provisions of such treaties will be judicially taken notice of by the courts of the nations who made the treaties, when occasion arises: and the forcible restraint applied to foreigners is guaranteed by the legal recognition of the validity of captures of slave-traders.

## § 6. *War.*

### A. *General Characteristics.*

The relation of peace is the result of the voluntary renunciation of complete national independence and isolation. The extreme case of the opposite of peace would occur if a nation were to repudiate that revocation and to take up with respect to all or any of its neighbours a position of absolute independence, refusing to recognise their corporate existence, to hold intercourse with their governments, to receive individuals belonging to them with hospitality, or to acquiesce in the application of their law to any of its own subjects under any circumstances. Such an extreme case is not likely to occur; if any nation did adopt such an attitude it would cease to be one of those states to which the name nation should be applied: if the position were long and successfully maintained it would mark the break-up of the national system and the introduction of some new phase in the history of mankind.

But it is possible for a nation without repudiating the whole to repudiate temporarily some part of the forbearances and concessions essential to the condition of peace, and by so doing to enter into the well-known and easily recognisable relation of war with any other nation. The possible causes of war are innumerable. One nation may go to war with another from a dislike of the laws which it administers, or from a belief that it administers them unfairly, or because the other nation appears to have shown bad faith in keeping a treaty, or because its government has failed to pay debts due to foreign individuals. War may at any time arise as the sanction in the last resort where a nation has violated the rules of international morality as they are understood by its neighbour. But most of the great wars which have taken place among nations have arisen from some wider and more general cause than any of these. War was the chief form of national activity which prevailed during the formation of the most ancient of the existing nations, and it received an enormous development at the time when the first great nations were finally launched on their independent careers. The desire for the acquisition of new territory, the desire for the development of commerce, the desire to spread or maintain particular religions, and the desire to increase the wealth and prosperity of the families which furnished the great European sovereigns, were the strongest motives in the minds of influential politicians whether on the throne or in the Council

Chamber. For every one of these ends war seemed a valuable means: and wars were accordingly the most conspicuous form of national life and ranked among the principal objects of the schemes and contrivances of statesmen.

The character of war, and the purposes for which it was waged, necessarily differed much from what they would have been, if the nations of Europe had come into the world complete, and had not very gradually emerged from the ruins of the Roman Empire. Many characteristics of the great wars from the 15th to the 18th century, especially during the early part of that period, and in those parts of Europe where the feudal system flourished longest, had their origin in the private wars of feudal times. In that pre-national era, war, which among nations is exclusively the concern of independent sovereign governments, was waged by potentates, and sometimes by lords low down in the feudal scale, who were subject for many purposes to political suzerainty. With the advance of time war came to be more and more a form of national activity. National policies and national ambitions became more complex. The idea of a nation as a great people, important from the number and character of its members rather than from the long descent and personal eminence of its ruler, began to exercise a strong influence on the policy of several nations. The enthusiasm for common ancestors, common traditions and a common language and literature, took their place as wide-spread influences on the members of nations, and modified the working of motives founded in commercial enterprise or territorial acquisition. To the desire for the propagation of a particular religion was added the desire for the propagation of political ideas or theories. As the life of nations became more complicated, and the threads of national policy more numerous and more tangled, the tendency to employ war as a means of giving effect to national ambition and increasing the importance of particular nations, did not decrease. The great wars of modern times have mostly resulted from the shock of the conflicting interests of nations, each of which was actuated by a number of ambitious theories and aspirations whose realisation it was the object of its government to achieve. Up to our own time great wars have had their real origin in such causes, and it seems rash to assert, though it has sometimes been asserted, that there will never again be a great war made for the purpose of giving consolidation and unity to a rising nation, of achieving a position of marked superiority for one of the leading nations of Europe, or of furthering or restraining national schemes of territorial acquisition and the instinct of "territorial expansion."

It seems advisable to insist a little on this topic because the students of international relations are so often called upon to consider war as the ultimate sanction employed by a nation which considers that its moral or quasi-legal rights in matters of detail have been violated, that they forget its historical importance as a regular phase of national activity.

War then is that relation, half-way from peace to barbaric isolation and unregulated violence, which springs up between two nations either because their political ambitions seem to conflict with one another, or because it is proved to the satisfaction of one of them that the derogations of the other from the standard of diplomatic propriety amount to a *casus belli*, or because one nation has made itself intolerably disagreeable to another in one of many possible ways.

But it is possible for a dispute between two nations to pass beyond the limits of peaceable diplomatic discussion without reaching the condition of war. A nation which authorises retorsion or the application of some harsh and unusual rules to the members of a nation by whom its members have been similarly treated, is already passing from the position of peaceable remonstrance in the direction of war. A more marked instance of the use of violent means of redress occurs where a nation authorises reprisals, or the violent seizure of a specified amount of property belonging to members of another nation, in satisfaction of debts or damages alleged to be due from that nation.

Another means of applying force to a foreign government is the institution of a pacific blockade. This practice consists in forcibly preventing access to the blockaded ports more or less nearly as in time of war, but without doing any other warlike acts or breaking off pacific relations with the power whose ports are blockaded. This practice can be resorted to with success only by a strong maritime power against a weak one: because effective retaliation by the blockaded power is almost certain to lead to a further state of international strife practically indistinguishable from war.

These various measures of violence falling short of war are similar in principle to intervention by way of threats or compulsory arbitration in the affairs of other nations, or between a foreign government and its temporarily revolted subjects. In all these cases the real nature of the transaction is this: a nation, actuated by some motives of policy or sentiment aroused by the facts of a particular case, determines to forego with respect to another nation some particular one or more of those concessions which go to make up the relation of peace: as for instance it ceases to leave it free to carry on its own commerce unhindered, or to settle questions of internal politics for itself. The means by which such a policy must be carried out do not necessarily go as far as setting up the relation of war: but the relation of war is very likely to come into existence very soon as the direct result of any one of these violent and unusual measures, and this has been found to be particularly true with respect to intervention.

The strongest possible instance of measures resembling war but to some extent falling short of it, occurs perhaps when a nation gives armed assistance to the sovereign of a revolted district, and puts down a rebellion otherwise likely to succeed by elaborate "military operations." In wars of colonial disruption or in civil wars where one party stigmatises the other as rebels, the recognition by neutral powers of alleged rebels as regular belligerents does not constitute any departure from the relation of peace, though like many other acts of a perfectly pacific character it may in particular cases give offence and embitter international relations: on the other hand, the recognition of the complete political independence of alleged rebels who are aiming at such independence but have not fairly established it beyond all possibility of doubt, is generally considered to be a departure from the respect normally shown to the independence of the government against whom the rebels have risen: such a respect is one of the elements of the relation of peace: and such premature recognition is therefore like a pacific blockade or an attempt at compulsory arbitration, a departure from the usual habits of international intercourse, in the direction of the abnormal relation of war, and one which is very likely to be followed by the outbreak of war.

All measures falling short of war but plainly departing from the usages of peace are necessarily liable to strong objections on the score of morality: but the incidents of international intercourse are so various, and such complicated conflicts of interest and sentiment may arise, that it seems impossible to lay down any general rules of morality, which could never be met by a complete answer founded on the facts of a particular case.

Little need be said about the mutual relations of two nations which are avowedly at war with one another. The relation of peace has been exchanged for one midway between peace and barbaric violence. The elements of that relation can be ascertained with tolerable accuracy from the study of past wars and of scientific treatises on the nature of war, but information accessible as to what any nation will do when it is at war can be best obtained by the study of the promises it has made by treaty and of the municipal laws which it has enacted with a view to the carrying-on of war. Every nation making war is subject to some extent to the influence of philanthropists, with whom war is unpopular for obvious reasons, and to arguments drawn from expediency and morality. At the same time the condition of war is one in which the immediate dictates of ambition and the pressure of mutual exasperation may at any given time outweigh all other motives and lead to the adoption of practices inconsistent with the ordinary conception of war and approximating to those which would mark a period of unrestrained rapacity and violence. Some of the practical sanctions of international morality are necessarily weakened by the existence of war: as those founded on the fear of violence from other nations would necessarily disappear in the extreme case of a nation already waging internecine war with a confederacy embracing all the nations which it had not reduced to complete submission, especially if the nation so situated appeared likely to bring its enterprise to a successful conclusion.

For the above reasons the actual elements of war cannot be strictly defined: though the truth as to what these elements ought to be according to the standard of morality has seemed to many writers to be more easily ascertainable. But some general facts about the practical nature of modern war can be safely laid down. It involves the breaking off of direct diplomatic intercourse between the belligerent nations, and of regular commercial relations between the individuals belonging to them. The chief object of war is the reduction of the enemy to an attitude of submission. This is effected on land by means of public military expeditions, for the destruction of his military resources, and the temporary occupation of his territory and towns: and at sea by a coöperation with land forces for the above purpose and by the interruption of his commerce. In a summary sketch it is impossible to treat in detail the extent of the common usage of belligerent nations with regard to the particular devices by which these processes are carried on, or the points upon which the usages of nations vary and international discussion arises. The nature of some of the questions incidental to such a discussion will appear from the topics of the laws mentioned in the next section; and some of the most important, and especially the practice of seizing private property at sea, are more nearly connected with the relation of belligerents to neutrals, than with that existing between belligerents. The questions of the circumstances under which a nation will make war, and the kind of terms which it will exact upon the successful termination of war, are questions of national policy, the decision of which must be regulated in accordance with circumstances of incalculable complexity. As to the amount of publicity to be given to the commencement of war, the treatment of obligations independent of the war itself, and the treatment of individuals belonging to a nation against which war is declared, but temporarily resident in the territory of the nation declaring war, the practice of nations is fairly uniform: it can be ascertained from the observation of actual wars, and is not to any great extent liable to the disturbing influence of novel considerations of policy.

### B. *Laws of International Import.*

There is only one class of laws which has direct reference to individuals belonging to foreign nations at war with the legislating nation. It consists of those laws which are made for the guidance of officers and soldiers engaged in warfare, in their conduct towards individuals belonging to a hostile army or to the hostile nation. These laws are exceptional in character not only because they are sometimes practically addressed to persons generally subject to another government, but also because they always refer to the conduct of individuals in places not ordinarily subject to the jurisdiction of the legislating government. An Englishman in France is generally subject to French and free from English jurisdiction. But an English soldier fighting in France is necessarily subject to English jurisdiction because during the continuance of war the jurisdiction and sovereignty of the territory which is the seat of war are habitually disregarded by the enemy.

Every nation must legislate expressly or tacitly for its soldiers and sailors on service. Such legislation creates a jurisdiction in places where there would otherwise be no jurisdiction, and enacts the rules to be enforced by the courts exercising such jurisdiction. In our own country, for instance, the Army Discipline Acts create certain military rights and duties, and the Articles of War, published under the legislative authority of those acts, give the sanction of municipal law to a more elaborate and detailed scheme for the regulation of the conduct of soldiers. Courts martial for the enforcement of military law sit under the sanctions of municipal law, and any irregularity in the constitution of such a court would be a matter for redress by legal process. Laws can be made authorising military commissions to deal with exceptional questions according to "the law of nations." The constitution of such commissions and the conditions of their efficiency are matters of municipal law, which further attaches a regular sanction, valid against individuals, to the opinion at which they may arrive as to the effect of the uncertain mass of opinion and usage indicated by the expression "law of nations."

In addition to this kind of law it is possible for courts of law to recognise the condition of war and supply their sanction to its effects by giving or refusing redress to persons who have suffered loss at the hands of a military or naval officer, acting under the orders of his government. The effect of the English law upon a question of this kind may be seen from the case of Buron *v.* Denman (*L. R.* 3 Exch. 167): and any matter which has been the subject of judicial decision in one country might be the subject of explicit legislation in all.

Only part of the regular military law of a nation possesses international import, or has such special reference to foreigners as to make the nature of its contents highly important to them. First, there are laws which in effect direct soldiers under regular sanctions to observe certain rules in their own behaviour towards the enemy. Secondly, there are laws which relieve from the regular legal responsibility soldiers who, in the course of military operations, use generally prohibited violence towards enemies who have committed specified offences. To take a rather complicated instance, a law may assert that bombardment without previous notice is not an international wrong: and one effect of this will be that if an enemy chooses to consider it as such a wrong and to retaliate by unusual acts of violence, the law will allow him to be treated in return as a person with regard to whose treatment the usual prohibitions do not apply. Thirdly, there are laws providing for the regular trial and punishment, by the means of specified judicial and executive machinery, of enemies who have committed specified offences.

It will suffice to enumerate a few of the topics with which these laws can deal. As an example we may consider the leading provisions of the *Instructions for the Government of Armies of the United States in the Field.* These Instructions were published by the supreme government of the United States in 1863: they are intended to supplement and interpret the laws already existing, whether statute law on military subjects or legislation empowering tribunals to exercise "the common law of war." The Instructions are in form (except so far as they deal with details of procedure) merely declaratory of a Law said to be universally binding on all the nations of the world. They are however of the nature of municipal law because they give a version of the common law, or it may be of the law of nations which is absolutely binding on the American courts which they create or to whose existence they refer. Therefore as far as these Instructions are explicit and complete the "law of nations" as incorporated into the law of America, and so furnished with sanctions applicable to individuals within American jurisdiction, has been authoritatively published.

The principal topics dealt with are as follows. An army which is in actual occupation of hostile territory is to administer martial law, or martial authority in accordance with the laws and usages of law, by means of organs established by municipal law, so far as such administration is necessary for the safety of the army and the success of its strategic schemes: in other respects the military authorities are to facilitate the administration in the ordinary way of the ordinary civil and penal law of the hostile nation. Rules are laid down for the treatment of consuls and of the diplomatic agents of neutral powers. Authority over the taxation and the police of the occupied territory is to be assumed as far as is required for the safety and efficiency of military operations. The regular means of carrying on war is to be by the destruction of the regular combatants of the enemy and by the starvation of enemies armed or unarmed and by the siege and bombardment of towns. Reasonable humanity must be used in the employment of these means. Retaliation against an enemy carrying on war by methods herein declared to be contrary to the "law of nations" is permissible in extreme cases. Rules are next laid down as to the extent to which the public property of the enemy is to be the subject either of permanent sequestration or temporary appropriation of the occupying army, and in particular with reference to charitable and scientific buildings. The military authorities are to make such arrangements as are practicable about the further employment and payment of the public officials of the occupied territory. Specified offences by American soldiers against the inhabitants of the occupied territory are to be punished by the military authorities. A slave escaping to an occupying army is to be considered as a slave escaping to the territory of the nation to which the army belongs. Detailed regulations are made as to who may become prisoners of war, what are to be the incidents of that condition of captivity, and how far the captors can take notice of previous offences committed by those who become prisoners. The circumstances under which the killing of prisoners or the refusal of quarter is criminal or justifiable are specified. Distinctions are made as to acts of legitimate deceit and acts of perfidy: and it is laid down that an enemy guilty of an act of perfidy may be made the subject of otherwise illegal violence with impunity. Elaborate provisions are made as to the treatment of enemies who occasionally take part in the war, without regularly belonging to the army of the enemy. An enemy who does acts of war without satisfying the conditions laid down as to sufficient enrolment or a distinctive dress is made liable to specified punishment at the hands of the army against whom he offends. The offence which consists in acting as a spy is defined and the punishment of death imposed upon those who are convicted of it. The whole subject of friendly intercourse between hostile armies is also the subject of detailed regulations. The proper employment of flags of truce, the conditions on which temporary truces or armistices are to be made, the validity of safe-conducts, and the means to be employed for the exchange or release of prisoners of war, are all guaranteed by legal rules bearing directly on American officers and soldiers and more or less indirectly on the individual enemies who take part in these transactions.

With regard to the various topics of which mention has been made it may be impossible to say what are the exact dictates of morality. Some of the questions of detail are of a very difficult nature, and they are not all of a character which all nations are likely to approach from exactly the same stand-point. But the value of more or less directly legal enactments on these topics consists in showing us what are the views of the legislating government as to the moral aspect of these questions, or at all events as to the particular modification of the moral doctrine which they propose to enforce by effectual means, against individuals who are subject to their control, or to that of the armies who recognise their authority.

## § 7. *Neutrality.*

### A. *General Characteristics.*

A nation is neutral in respect of any war in which it does not take part. The importance attached to the condition of neutrality has increased and the complicated nature of its elements has appeared owing to the multiplication of the commercial relations subsisting between members of different nations and to the fact that war has become a well-understood relation of which the general results upon the belligerents can be pretty accurately foreseen.

The object of a neutral government is to keep its relations with the belligerent nations as nearly as possible undisturbed by the existence of the war. The object of a belligerent government is to secure the perfect impartiality of neutral powers and to be as little hampered as possible by neutrals in carrying on the recognised operations of warfare.

A neutral government is likely to resent any use for purposes of war of its territory, or of that part of the sea which it treats as part of its territory for military purposes: and it wishes as far as possible to continue in safety its commercial dealings with either belligerent. A belligerent government is likely to resent any use by the enemy of neutral territory, men or materials for military purposes, and to object to any support being given by neutrals to the enemy either directly or by assistance to their commercial enterprises.

Belligerents and neutrals, being actuated by such conflicting motives, have often quarrelled about the conduct which they ought to pursue towards one another. Such quarrels have taken every form, from the slightest to the most severe, of international remonstrance and strife. When such difficulties have been avoided it has been owing to the adoption by the two parties of some compromise which strikes an average between these conflicting interests, or leans more nearly to one or the other according to the comparative strength at the time of belligerents and neutrals.

A belligerent government is pretty sure to excite resentment in a neutral government, and to meet with the general disapproval of nations, if the public forces under its control actually carry on military operations on the territory or in the territorial waters subject to the authority of the neutral government: the same result will follow any attempt by a belligerent government to interfere with persons or property on board a neutral ship under circumstances other than those specified in the following section, or the adoption by a belligerent government of unusually harsh and stringent rules in its relations with neutral individuals. A neutral government will incur similar resentment and disapprobation if it allows its territory to serve as a base of operations against a belligerent, if it encourages or entirely fails to restrain or discountenance expeditions organised by its subjects for the purpose of assisting a party to the war, or if it allows its subjects to supply material of war upon a large scale to one of the contending parties. It is impossible to ascertain the exact point at which such a contribution of materials would be considered to be on a sufficiently large scale to lead to the neutral government being held responsible: but it is unquestionable that circumstances of this kind can arise which would lead to a quarrel between the belligerent government and the neutral government. The history of the Alabama claim, the arguments on which the decision of the arbitrators on that occasion was based, and the language employed by a great number of writers on international relations in the discussion of this topic, show that a very strong body of opinion would support a belligerent government complaining against a neutral government for allowing or not preventing the supply of warlike materials on a large scale, and especially the building, arming and sending out of ships intended to take part in the war. Another ground of complaint by a belligerent against a neutral government would be the refusal by the latter to acquiesce in the application by the former of such laws as it may have more or less formally enacted to prevent or punish assistance given on a comparatively small scale by neutral individuals to the enemies of the belligerent government.

With the above exceptions the relation of neutrality is not likely to lead to differences or complications between neutral and belligerent governments: but it leads to many kinds of questions between belligerent governments and neutral individuals, which are the subject of laws and which therefore belong to the next section.

### B. *Laws of International Import.*

There are two kinds of legislation of international import having special reference to the relation of neutrality. Members of a nation are restrained from taking part in a war to which the nation is not a party, first, by laws enforced by the sovereign power to which they are subject: secondly, by laws enforced against them by the foreign belligerent government.

A legislature which has the condition of neutrality in view may make laws to restrain its subjects from any one of those kinds of conduct which constitute an interference in war at the expense of a foreign belligerent. In practice such legislation has only recently been known among nations to at all a large extent: and it is now confined to a very few of the possible ways of assisting a belligerent. In the case of England, for instance, the Foreign Enlistment Act of 1818 made it a punishable offence for a British subject to accept a commission from a foreign government in time of war or to take part directly in such a war in various other ways. The Foreign Enlistment Act of 1870 renews this prohibition with greater stringency and elaboration, especially as to the fitting out of ships intended to be used in a foreign war. Such legislation as this is due to the anxiety of the legislating government either to restrain its subjects from a course which it holds to be of that kind of immorality which may be properly made illegal, or to avoid the resentment of belligerent powers whose enemies have employed the services of neutrals as soldiers or ship-builders, and the important practical results of such resentment. Laws of various kinds may be enacted in different nations to secure the objects aimed at by the Foreign Enlistment Acts: but it is not usual, though it would be perfectly possible, for governments to forbid their subjects to minister to the requirements of belligerents by means other than the supply of men or ships.

These other matters are generally the subject of the second class of laws of which we have spoken: laws enforced by a belligerent government against individuals subject to a foreign government and within foreign jurisdiction at the time of doing the acts prohibited. These laws deal principally with assistance given to an enemy who is being attacked through his commerce. They embrace such matters as the carriage of enemy's goods in neutral ships, the supply of contraband of war, and the breach of blockade.

These matters have sometimes been the subject of unmistakable legislation, as by the ordinances on maritime law of the early Italian republics and of the French kings. In England and the United States, the two nations whose policy with respect to neutral rights has perhaps had the widest importance, owing to the strength of their maritime position, the fact that municipal laws have been laid down and enforced for the regulation of the conduct of foreigners has not been generally admitted either by writers on international relations or by the courts which have themselves enforced those laws. It might however be shown that the English and American prize courts, in dealing with the rights and duties of neutrals have in fact administered English and American law. Like other parts of the common law of England, the law administered by the English prize-court judges during England's great maritime wars was not to be found in any definite enactments of the legislature; but it was law because the authority of the executive could be utilised for its enforcement, so that it was tacitly accepted by the sovereign authority. It is true that the judges of the prize courts often stated that it was their duty and their intention to administer not the law of England but the general law of nations. At the same time there are passages in their judgments which show that they did sometimes look upon themselves as administering English law. They explicitly asserted with respect to some topics that the law of nations was to such or such an effect: and that the law of England was that the law of nations should be followed, except in cases where it was to be modified on account of particular treaties of which the court took judicial cognisance, or by the fact that the government whose subjects were at the moment before the court was in the habit of applying to English subjects some rule different to that of the Law of Nations. This seems to be the true view of the nature of prize courts. It is possible to collect from the decisions of judges what is the law which they in fact administer with the assistance of the sovereign authority of their own nation. The reason of their adoption of the rules which they administer is in many cases a belief that these rules are in fact part of the universal law of nations. But the actual nature of the alleged law of nations has always been a matter of uncertainty: and in times of great European discord belligerent nations and neutral nations have differed as to its actual contents, partly on account of interested motives from which even judges are not wholly free. The shortest and plainest way of summing up the matter seems to be as follows: in time of war it is usual for nations to give to courts of their own, jurisdiction over the captors and owners of neutral ships and property taken at sea. These courts apply to the question of the validity of any such capture practical rules of law which can be ascertained from the study of their decisions. There is no reason why these rules should not be formulated and, if it were thought wise, amended by means of regular municipal legislation: and if this were done it might increase the simplicity of the laws of different nations on these subjects, and tend to produce uniformity.

Assuming then that the law administered by prize courts is of the nature of municipal law, we may briefly summarise the principal kinds of laws which can be made by a belligerent government and administered against neutral individuals.

In the first place laws have often been made for the forfeiture of contraband of war. Under this name it has been usual to include all such merchandise being conveyed to a belligerent port as is obviously and necessarily intended to be used as munition of war and such other kinds of merchandise as appear, owing to the particular circumstances of a war or of any phase of a war, to be likely to be used for military purposes. It has been found exceedingly difficult to draw up an accurate list of the kinds of merchandise which are contraband: and in this, as in other matters, courts determined to adopt or incorporate the "Law of Nations" have differed considerably as to what is the actual view of that law on the question. On this, as on all the kindred topics, courts of law have incorporated and enforced the rules laid down by treaty to be observed towards particular states except when the treaty is of very old date or has been frequently disregarded by the other power or powers agreeing to it. The public ships of belligerent governments have generally been allowed to bring in ships containing any contraband cargo to a port of the belligerent nation, in order to have the legal question decided by a prize court: and such part of the cargo as is declared to be contraband has been forfeited to the captors. Laws allowing the forfeiture of the ship and of the innocent part of the cargo have been rare and unpopular.

A second instance consists in the laws on the subject of blockaded ports. The laws enforced by most nations on this subject have proceeded on the general principle that where a ship belonging to a neutral attempts to enter a harbour which is practically and undoubtedly invested by belligerent ships with a view to depriving the town of supplies and so forcing it to surrender, the ship and cargo are both forfeited to the captor. Laws have also been made enforcing some lighter penalty. But the great difference between the laws of different nations on the subject of blockade has been as to what facts constitute a blockade in the legal sense. Some nations have acted on the view that there is always a blockade when certain conditions are fulfilled, as for instance that there shall be not less than a specified number of ships stationary during a given time within a given distance of the entrance to the harbour. Others have maintained that general rules are impracticable, and that it is a question for the court upon every set of facts that may arise whether the principle of sufficient investment is or is not satisfied by those facts. The question of blockade is one with regard to which it is specially true that the law, whether as practically administered or as explicitly enacted in a particular nation, may develope rapidly in the direction of severity under the pressure of a prolonged war and of the mutual exasperations inherent in its progress. There is a tendency at such times to extend the practical results of blockade to cases in no way falling under the general principle usually governing the matter. The strongest instance of this is to be found in Napoleon's celebrated decree by which the British isles were declared to be in a state of blockade, and all neutral commerce with them was forbidden. This is a strong instance of what may always happen in this kind of legislation at unusually troubled times. A nation which believes or professes to believe that it has to deal with an enemy of the human race, and which occupies an unusually favourable position for the enforcement of its will against its neighbours, is likely to administer a different law from that which it has enacted and enforced in quieter times. When the Scandinavian powers were the only neutrals in Europe they truly complained upon several occasions that the members of the coalition against Napoleon were dealing out a different measure to neutrals from that which they had previously declared to be the "Law of Nations": and they were met by an answer which amounted in substance to this—that the powers which had formerly incorporated what they believed to be the "Law of Nations" into their own laws, were now compelled by unprecedented circumstances, which made the very condition of neutrality immoral, to adopt in place of that portion of their laws something which differed from the "Law of Nations."

A subject on which the laws, explicit and tacit, of different nations have varied considerably from one another is that of the treatment of hostile cargo on board neutral ships. The fluctuations of legislation on this topic cannot be here traced. It will be sufficient to say that in most great maritime wars the belligerent powers have adopted the rule that enemy's property on board hostile ships is liable to capture: but that at the present time the principal nations have promised each other by treaty to treat such property (where there is no question of contraband or of blockade-running) as free from capture, and that prize courts would probably give a practical effect to a rule that this promise should be observed, unless their attitude and policy were changed by exceptional international aggravation or other disturbing circumstances.

A kindred subject of legislation has been the treatment of neutral goods found on board hostile ships: on this subject the more tolerant view has been accepted and enforced by the courts of nations generally the least favourable to neutrals, but the opposite view has also found judicial and legislative support.

In nations where there has been a great quantity of judge-made law on international topics, very elaborate rules and subtle distinctions have been constructed as to the exact meaning of the expressions "enemy's ship" and "enemy's goods" and as to the evidence which will establish the hostile character of a ship or cargo and the acts of fraud or bad faith which will give rise to a presumption of hostility. The rules which different nations have enforced on these very delicate questions, and on the exact results which follow upon the proof of the various kinds and degrees of hostility, can only be ascertained from a careful and detailed examination of judicial dicta and decisions, precisely similar to that by which the more difficult problems of the English common law and on the interpretation of statutes, must be decided.

Various rules have at different times been laid down or suggested for the forfeiture or apprehension of goods or of individuals under the control of neutrals, when the carriage or protection of them seemed to be especially calculated to assist one belligerent at the expense of the other, although the particular case might not fall under any of the recognised heads of blockade, contraband, hostile merchandise, etc. But the kinds of legislation above summarised are those which have appeared the most frequently and regularly and which have had the greatest importance.

The laws concerning this class of international relations cannot be carried out without the visitation and more or less formal search by the public ships of belligerents of the private ships of neutrals. The public ships of neutrals have generally been held exempt from such search. A rule commonly enforced, but which has given rise to considerable complaints and to diplomatic difficulties, sanctions the capture and entire forfeiture of such private ships as, under any circumstances, resist such visitation or refuse to give the desired information to the public ships of belligerents.

A rule of law at one time enforced in the English courts, but which it would now most likely be impossible to support successfully, was that which treated as hostile, and therefore liable to capture, any neutral vessel which engaged in the coasting trade of the belligerent, or in trade with the colonies of the belligerent if such trade was forbidden to foreigners in ordinary times and only thrown open to them under the pressure of the war.

In addition to the questions arising between a belligerent government and neutral individuals there are certain questions arising between a belligerent government and the members of a nation allied to it in time of war, which are the subject of laws. The most important of these is the question of the length of time which renders capture of the ally's ship by the enemy complete, so as to give to a subject of the other ally who rescues the captured ship a good title against the original owner; and in close connection with this is the amount of salvage due to the rescuer in cases where the captured ship is returned. Most nations have some definite law to determine the length of the period and the amount of the salvage among their own subjects: and the commonest rule as to allies is that which applies that law, whatever it is, to the rescued ships of allies, unless the ally has observed a different rule towards the subjects of the legislating nation.

It will be observed that all the kinds of law relating to neutrality which have been mentioned refer to neutral individuals taking part directly or indirectly in a war. Of course this subject, whether from the harsh nature of the laws of a particular nation or from any other reason, may lead to diplomatic disputes, changes of policy, and war. The other kind of breaches of neutrality, where a belligerent trespasses on neutral territory for the purposes of the war to the prejudice of the neutral, are not so often the subject of legal redress and are more likely to lead to directly international complications. But when such violations of neutral territory are made the subject of legal proceedings, application of forcible restraint by the neutral, the municipal character of the law administered is obvious, as the offence then dealt with is a breach of the peace within the ordinary jurisdiction of the neutral. The commonest way, however, in which law has been brought to bear on violations of neutral territory is by the refusal of a belligerent's prize court to give practical validity to the capture of hostile ships within neutral territory. The part of a neutral government upon such an occasion is confined to diplomatic representations and the assertion of particular views on the question of morality, with the usual threats.

A neutral government may give offence to a belligerent government by not strictly enforcing those of its laws against breaches of its neutrality of which the violation injures the belligerent: but such grievances, being against a foreign government, are generally the subject not of law but of diplomatic remonstrance and more or less declared hostility.

CAMBRIDGE: PRINTED BY C. J. CLAY, M.A. & SON, AT THE UNIVERSITY PRESS.

CPSIA information can be obtained
at www.ICGtesting.com
Printed in the USA
LVOW13s1620070217
523494LV00010B/713/P

9 780554 885551